MARIE JENNINGS
AND DAVID CHURCHILL

CW01498581

GETTING
MESSAGE ACROSS

A GUIDE TO DIRECTING
CORPORATE COMMUNICATIONS

PUBLISHED IN ASSOCIATION WITH
THE INSTITUTE OF DIRECTORS

DIRECTOR BOOKS

Published by Director Books,
an imprint of Fitzwilliam Publishing Limited,
Simon & Schuster International Group,
Fitzwilliam House, 32 Trumpington Street,
Cambridge CB2 1QY, England

First published 1988
© Marie Jennings and David Churchill 1988

Conditions of sale
All rights reserved. No part of this publication may be reproduced, stored in a
retrieval system or transmitted, in any form or by any means, electronic, mechanical,
photocopying, recording or otherwise, without the prior permission of the publisher.

The Council of the Institute of Directors
accepts no responsibility for opinions expressed
by the authors.

British Library Cataloguing in Publication Data
Jennings, Marie
Getting the message across.
1. Business firms. Management.
Communication. Manuals.
I. Title   II. Churchill, David
III. Institute of Directors.
658.4'5

ISBN 1-87055-06-6

Designed by Geoff Green
Typeset by Hands Fotoset, Leicester
Printed in Great Britain by A. Wheaton and Co. Ltd, Exeter

GETTING THE MESSAGE ACROSS

FOREWORD

Sir John Hoskyns, Director General, Institute of Directors

Managing the communications function – getting the message across

GREATER professionalism and skill in the performance of every business function must be the objective of British companies, large and small, if they are to be successful and play their part in the country's economic recovery. No board of directors would contemplate employing other than the most experienced, best qualified people to advise them on financial management, legal affairs, sales or industrial relations.

More and more businessmen are coming to appreciate that another vital management role – communication – must be added to the list of skills which require the professional touch. For communication, in all its forms – public relations, advertising, marketing, employee involvement – is becoming increasingly important to the image, performance and profitability of businesses.

Many large companies are already aware of the key part communication has to play and have their own in-house public relations departments or employ outside agencies and consultants. For the small or medium-sized business, however, creating the right image to its customers, suppliers and employees can be expensive and time-consuming. And whatever the size of the company, selecting the most appropriate, cost-effective method of 'getting the message across', from the myriad of options, can be a make-or-break decision. It can assure success, or doom a product or service to failure.

We are in an age of increasing competition and entrepreneurial activity in which professional advice on how to maximize a company's production and marketing effort is no longer a luxury but an essential weapon in the armoury of management. Companies need expert guidance to assess the merits of a public relations promotion as compared with the value of an advertising campaign; how proper research can further their sales and when careful lobbying of opinion-formers and influential journalists can enhance their prospects of success. No company can afford to ignore internal communications with its employees, and there is strong evidence that businesses which have given importance to this have seen tangible benefits both in terms of performance and competitiveness. Public relations is no longer merely a matter of putting out a press release, organizing exhibitions, demonstrations or seminars. It is an art, in which the video, graphic design and new technology printing methods have created a requirement for specialized skills.

Marie Jennings and David Churchill have a wealth of experience in all the skills of the communication practitioner. They have brought their expertise together in this book to provide a timely and much-needed work of reference to guide the company director and business manager. Their objective has been to provide guidance for all businesses, but the book will be of particular value to developing and expanding companies which are perhaps in the position of becoming 'first-time buyers' of the services of public relations consultants or advertising agencies.

The authors provide a yardstick on the likely cost of employing consultants and illuminate their book with case studies of company experience. For the businessman who is interested in saving time and effort, and getting value for money, they have produced a piece of essential reading.

ACKNOWLEDGEMENTS

THE authors wish to express thanks to Roger Haywood, David Fleming, Brian Locke, Sally Buxton, Mandy Williams and Colin Thompson (Secretary General of the Public Relations Consultants Association) for their assistance with the preparation of this book.

CONTENTS

❦

INTRODUCTION

❧

Why this book?

As a director you already have what you probably consider is too much paper flowing across your desk, endless meetings to attend and broadcasts of one sort or another to listen to. 'Why', you may well ask, 'another book about communication? And do I really have to read it? I think I am pretty familiar with the subject already.'

But are you? You may be all too familiar with the end results of communications – with all the paper, the media reports, the endless surveys, analyses, management reports, sales figures, forecasts, projections, one-year, three-year, and five-year corporate and business plans, informal and formal meetings. But how much time have you spent really examining some of the philosophical, planning, managerial and practical implications of communication? That is what this book is all about.

Why should you read it? Because today communication is without doubt the thorniest subject any director has to deal with. All directors have to handle it – every employee, customer, shareholder, owner or opinion-former is exposed to it. Because, quite simply, it is no good doing well if people are not aware of it. No organization, large or small, can say that it is really satisfied with its record and that it cannot do better. Every tier in the organization is involved. The need for understanding, planning and action surrounds the director on all sides.

This book is attempting to look at the subject of communication in a slightly different way. It is trying to cut through the mass of words and jargon to harness thinking, to present a simple, practical guide to the reader on corporate communication.

We, the authors, have different backgrounds, with different

perceptions and writing styles. David Churchill, a distinguished commentator from the media, has observed the evolution of the practices used in business to communicate messages. Marie Jennings, journalist and public affairs specialist, has taken an active role, through working with the Public Relations Consultants Association, towards signposting to business the advantages that lie in giving more priority to the overall area of communication. She has been campaigning for developing means of evaluation to show business the value for money equation in relation to good communication. The aim of this book is to provide some basic information about communication and how it could and should affect your business. Then we discuss how you should look at the practice of communication in your organization and how it can be managed. We give you some practical case histories, and tell you where to get help if you need it. Perhaps, more important, we have tried to put together some thoughts which we hope will help you to widen the horizons of your understanding of total communication. In general the subject is considered in the context of the United Kingdom, but most of the points made are relevant internationally. Let us try to set the scene:

The four cornerstones of all communication

1. The recognition that communication is an ongoing process – it is happening all the time. 'Messages' of many different sorts are going out and being received. Nothing can be done to stop the process. You are giving impressions of your business to all the target audiences of that business – all the time. Employees, customers, intermediaries, shareholders, people in the local community, all have an impression about your business, about its image and corporate identity, about its management, about the products or services in which you trade, and also about you – as a manager, as a director of the organization and also, of course, as a person, as an individual.

   The impressions you are giving are directly related to what you are doing about them, and how well you understand the position. Do nothing and the impressions can vary from bad to diabolical, and if they are anything more than the latter, then you are very, very lucky! Do a lot, plan carefully, implement effectively and you could be surprised at the reward in real terms.

2. The timing of the message. Plan ahead – public recognition of any

change or development of the message you are giving out takes time. Radical changes take, naturally, even more time. Add in the planning process, and the whole sequence, from initial idea to reaction by the target audience, places communication squarely under the heading of 'long-term planning'. Often an organization changes its messages, but does not reflect in the planning the timing necessary to ensure that the message gets through and can achieve the company's objectives.

3. The understanding of the message. What you may believe, or mean to say to your target audience, is really of no consequence at all. It is the message that is being received which is of paramount importance. It is how your message is interpreted and acted upon that really matters. Is this recognized within your organization?

4. The response to the message. It has to be recognized that most people reject a large proportion of the messages they are receiving all day, every day. In truth they only absorb a very small proportion. As a director of your company, are you allowing for this?

Food for thought?

To these four cornerstones on communication, let us now add some mortar or cement – recognition of the fact that resistance to communication exists in us all, all the time. As with a building, the architect has to take into consideration the stresses and strains which the building will have to endure from different weather conditions, so in communication you will also have to take into consideration different levels of resistance and prejudice. You must allow for levels of prejudice which may exist in the person to whom you are directing your message. You need to examine and plan the means of overcoming that prejudice. You need to allow for the time it takes to overcome that prejudice. It could easily take half a generation (approximately 12 years) to achieve significant success if it relates to a shift in attitude in a large organization. Substantial changes in attitude in larger numbers of people, in the general public, could easily take a generation – or more.

Remember, too, that in most companies communication moves backwards and forwards, it doesn't move up and down, and it should. Allow for this. Allow, too, for the communication of the business ethos, as well as the particular message.

One final thought for this introduction. It is very simple, but often forgotten.

Actions speak louder than words.

So when you are communicating, do so in conjunction with some action, however small, just as often as possible.

Sir John Harvey-Jones, a former chairman of ICI, has talked of the two simple priorities a business leader has to remember at all times: the responsibility to listen, sensitively, the responsibility to communicate effectively with all tiers in the organization, to be in touch, and to remain in touch. That applies as much outside the organization as well as within it.

This is what effective corporate communication is all about. We hope that you will find this book useful. We have enjoyed writing it, and we hope it will prove an aid to improved corporate communications.

Marie Jennings
David Churchill

CHAPTER 1

CORPORATE COMMUNICATIONS
AND THE COMPANY

ℰ≈℈

THE fact is, you are already deeply involved in a programme of corporate communication whether you like it or not. However well or ill-considered, however much or little of your management's time is involved, your company communicates information about itself. It is the same with your competitors. They need not even speak your company's name; their actions, their use of technology, their distribution, represent the changing criteria against which your own company is judged.

Since this book's purpose is to act as a practical guidebook through the corporate communications jungle, the following illustration may provide some ideas. During 1979 to 1981 Intel and Motorola were fighting for the micro-processor market. Intel prepared a *Futures Catalog*, a detailed description of products it was working on, but had not yet launched. In reply, Motorola rushed out its own catalogue, which seemed much inferior. As William Davidow, who masterminded Intel's campaign, reports: 'Ultimately, the Motorola catalog became an Intel sales tool, possibly the best one we had'.[1]

So, one question which this book will not address is whether your company should be involved in a full-time, 24-hour day, corporate communication programme – because it is anyway, without being able to help it. The question it will address is how to make that campaign work to your company's advantage. And the answer to that, the message of this book, can be summarized in four words: *Don't add on, integrate.*

In other words, corporate communication and corporate strategy, like two blades of a pair of scissors, are part of a single system. They work together.

The complete product

'We're known by our brands. Why does the customer need to know about our company?' This question, and the implication that the identity of the company itself does not matter very much, so long as the products are in good shape, is a very common one. And so indeed is the usual answer – that the product is not all that matters, and that a company fails to communicate to its other audiences too, such as shareholders, employees and potential recruits, at its peril.

However, that answer is the wrong one, for two reasons. First, it does not distinguish between the radically different communication needs of different companies. It is true that some highly successful companies in the consumer field are almost unknown to their customers. Procter and Gamble, for example, which sells almost £500 million-worth of consumer goods in the United Kingdom, is known to its customers almost exclusively by its brands. One of the most successful high street groups, C & A, has made a strategy of corporate secrecy for many years. Many low-value goods from the Far East, such as ball-point pens, are sold in this country in a climate of almost total ignorance about their source of supply.

So, a 'low profile' in corporate communication, while it may be far from ideal, has at least in some instances a presentable track record. A single prescription is no more appropriate in the field of corporate communication than it would be in medicine.

Secondly, the stock answer is wrong because it does not go anywhere near far enough. A properly-constructed corporate communications programme is necessary for any company that wishes to sell *a complete product*.[2]

Focusing on the basic relationship between seller and buyer, and leaving the case of shareholders, employees and other audiences until later in this chapter, the following instances have been chosen to make the contrasts as clear as possible.

1. *A powerful mainframe computer.* In this instance, the customer is buying a serious long-term relationship with the supplier. He is buying a service contract and a guarantee, so he needs to know that the supplier is financially sound and will continue to be in business for the foreseeable future and that the supplier's service department is reliable and easy to work with. He needs to be reassured that the supplier's research and development is up with the leaders in the field, so that when the computer becomes obsolete he can replace it with an updated version from the same company,

avoiding problems of incompatibility between the two systems.

Perhaps most important of all, in this situation, the customer needs to be reassured that the supplier is a well-known and respected firm, so that if anything does go wrong, the customer's own colleagues will not blame him for having made a risky choice.

These are the main reasons, of course, why IBM has fought off the competition for market leadership in the computer market, despite being overtaken technologically over and over again by less well-known competitors. The smaller companies could offer better technology, but only IBM could offer the *complete product*.

With the example of the computer market as a benchmark, the others follow without difficulty.

2. *A ball-point pen*. Minimal information is required. The product can be tried and thrown away almost without cost. The product is without significant risks or longevity. It is complete, without additional information or reassurance.

3. *Office construction*. The developer does not buy a product; instead, he bets on his judgement and evaluation of the contractor's service. For the contractor, corporate communications and marketing are identical. The company is the brand.

4. *Detergent*. This is not, like the ball-point pen, a simple product, and it cannot be immediately assessed. It may be good, or it may be ineffective, a health hazard, or an environmental hazard; or it may be associated with positive or negative emotions, reassuring or challenging, friendly or strange. The complete product consists of a set of material qualities and emotional associations which fit into the image of a brand, but do not sit easily with that of a company, which may be the source of a range of products with sharply different associations. In this case the brand itself takes on much of the communication role of the company.

Here, then, is the first way in which corporate communication and corporate strategy form part of a single system. The question to consider is, 'What is the complete product?' and the answer to that can be plotted in Fig. 1.1. The left-hand axis represents the extreme cases of the commodity, as in the case of the ball-point pen, and the brand, as in the case of the detergent. These are situations in which the customer's view of the company is only minimally relevant to his or her attitude to the brand. At any point to the right of these extreme cases, corporate communication forms a direct and (as we move nearer to the right-hand axis) critical component of *marketing*.

Fig. 1.1 The complete product: the company-brand communication mix.

The communication of strategy

The 'complete product' is, of course, only half the story. Even if the product is completely marketed, the company itself must work in an environment in which customers in their various roles, as shareholders and employees, local authorities, potential recruits, consumer and environmental groups, parent and subsidiary companies, competitors, suppliers, consultants and banks – to name but a few of the groups whose opinions and actions matter to a company – affect a company in such a way as to assist, or to impede or even destroy it.

So, a company has a communication programme which it directs to these audiences, and the job is delegated to a public relations department or consultancy. But what on earth does it say? We do not pollute the environment? We are good people to work for? We hope our price-earnings ratio will be higher before too long? We love wildlife?

This is the problem of the communication programme becoming

split from the corporate strategy. There are many brilliant books on corporate strategy, but in most the word 'communication' does not even appear in the index. In the books on corporate communication, the word 'strategy' is similarly missing. So we need to look at the matter afresh.

After the launch of the Mazda car in the United Kingdom, one public relations executive was summoned to Japan by Toyo Kogyo to report on its press reception. He was taken straight from the plane to the factory, where he turned over the newspaper clippings, with adverse comments heavily circled, and discussed them with Mazda executives. He was then allowed to check into his hotel to sleep. The next morning, returning to the factory, he found a prototype incorporating changes designed to meet the press criticisms.

This story, which is quoted in Robert Heller's *The Supermarketers*,[3] gives a flavour of the urgency, the sense of being on a 'war footing', which is characteristic of present-day business strategy. Heller's book reads in places like the screenplay for a war movie. On the battle between IBM and Compaq, for instance, he writes:

> Frontal assault is . . . impossible; the challenger must find a way round. The Compaq outflankers were recruited in the obvious place – two heroes of IBM's own fabled PC launch were poached – and they identified the Achilles' heel of their former employer. . .
>
> 'If you're growing slowly, problems can sidle up on you almost unnoticed,' argues Compaq president Rod Canion. 'With high growth, if you don't get out of the way first, they knock you down flat.'

In a competitive climate like this, no one will see the value of corporate communication if it is regarded as a luxury, away from the fray. But it is no more a peripheral activity than is the company's strategy itself; it is nothing less than the strategy's medium, its voice.

The techniques of strategic development are familiar to most large company directors and certainly to all business school graduates. The first step is the strategic analysis, with its evaluation of the firm's environment, its resources, the value systems of its stakeholders – the many groups, ranging from employees to shareholders, indeed all who have a stake in the organization – and the expectations of the stakeholders. Then strategic options are drawn up and chosen, so that the third step in the cycle is strategic implementation.[4]

That, at least, is the textbook approach, and the only thing it leaves out is the creative drive of an effective top management: because, first and last, the corporate strategy depends on the insight and imagination of the company's leadership. The firm asks different questions, makes different demands of its stakeholders, selects as significant different features of its environment, in the light of its corporate plan.

But does the strategy identify and define the company? It does not. The strategy stays on the drawing board until it is communicated. And since the whole set of stakeholders is involved in some way in the implementation of the company's strategy, the communication programme could be complex indeed. In Fig. 1.2, 15 different groups of stakeholders are identified; if each stakeholder group receives some form of message, derives some information about the company, from another group (and this kind of spillover between groups is normal), that implies a potential confusion of over 200 messages back and forth between the groups; and each message may be slightly or sharply in discord with another.

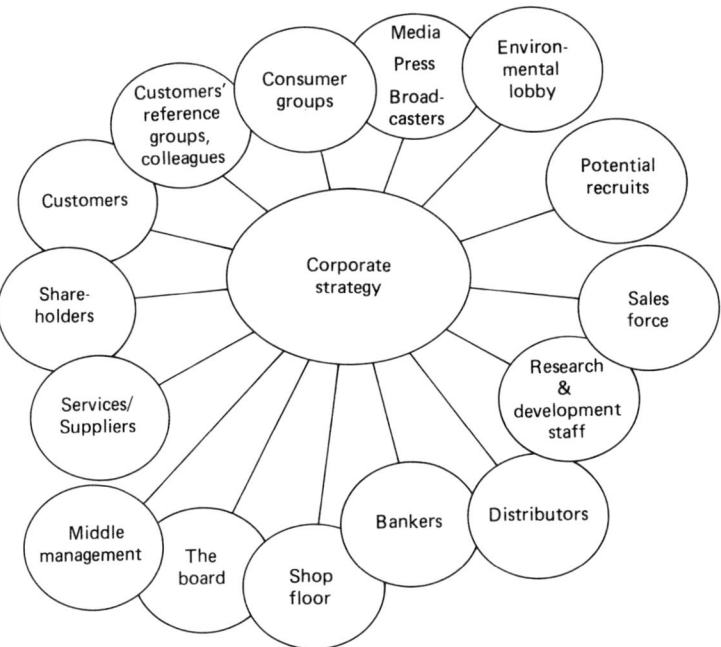

Fig. 1.2 Examples of stakeholders: relations with the many different audiences surrounding a company may be organized by a coherent corporate strategy.

On the other hand, if the company strategy is clearly defined and communication among the stakeholder groups reflects this, then we have the makings of an effective organization, one whose sense of direction is not confined to the boardroom, but which, to use military terminology for one last time, is an 'effective fighting machine'.

But what about social responsibility, you may ask, consumer relations, help lines, being a good neighbour? These are indeed the heart of the matter. If such considerations are inconsistent with the corporate strategy, that strategy is wrong.

This then, is what is meant by integration. Good communications are not a policy option; they are the criteria for an effective corporate strategy.

Dialogue and dissonance

Shell's varied fortunes in corporate advertising in 1973–80 have turned into one of the standard case studies of corporate communication. In 1973, with the Arab oil embargo, motorists had the unwelcome experience of having to queue for their petrol. In 1974, the oil companies reported improved profits, and they were openly accused of cheating the public. The fact that the improvement in profits was due to price controls imposed by the United States government did nothing to allay the criticism. [5]

Shell responded with a corporate advertising campaign. It showed Shell's ships bucketing through rough seas to oil rigs. It was called 'People Working with Energy'. The other major oil companies also launched advertising campaigns showing their ships bucketing through rough seas to oil rigs. Viewers called the advertising campaigns 'Victory at Sea', and drew from them further evidence that the oil companies were acting in collusion. The public estimation of Shell and the oil industry sank from indifference to dislike.

Shell then carried out some very intensive market research, and rethought the problem. It produced a new set of corporate advertising objectives:

1. Enhance Shell's reputation for responsible behaviour.
2. Contribute to the credibility of Shell's representatives and statements.
3. Support Shell's claim of excellence in products, services and people.
4. Favourably differentiate Shell from other major oil companies. The strategy for achieving this was to demonstrate Shell's responsiveness to *consumer* needs by providing useful consumer information.

The campaign focused on the last, and most important, segment of the strategy; it provided advice on a range of aspects of motoring, developed the theme 'Come to Shell for answers', and produced a series of *Shell Answer Books*, many of which have been adopted as core teaching material for driving instruction. Shell had already established a reputation over many years as producers of useful public interest books and this became, by a wide margin, the top-ranking oil company in terms of public estimation, and much of the criticism of the industry as a whole was defused.

There are three messages to be drawn from this case study. First, it clarifies the concept of the 'complete product'; petrol is not, in our terms, a product; it is a chemical. The product is made up of the full spectrum – the company's services, the sense that the consumer is buying from a responsible and helpful organization, the sense that the supplier is interested in the customer, and not just in macho marine heroics. Corporate communication? Product communication? The distinction is meaningless. With that campaign, Shell matured further along the path from dealer in inflammable liquids, to effective marketing company. It became a real communicator.

Secondly, the study illustrates the way in which strategy and communication can and must be integrated. Shell did not merely claim that it was concerned with social responsibility and working with the consumer; it did not buy an 'I love the consumer' lapel badge. It actually shifted its strategy first, built a platform of genuine consumer service, and allowed the consumer to draw his and her own conclusions.

Thirdly, it illustrates the final message of this chapter: if you want to communicate effectively, the first thing to do is to listen; and in the light of that, keep the communication sharply focused.

There is more to the matter of focusing a campaign than mere economy of effort. An exact perception of any company by any of its stakeholders is good in parts and bad in parts; competing companies' product lines are incomplete in different ways; consumers' environments are a network of trade-offs and compromises. To make sense of this complexity, people simplify. They select some of the main characteristics of a situation, and allow that to colour their whole attitude. From this it follows that a company does not have to claim to be on the side of the angels in every aspect of its activities. It needs to focus only on one important and telling message, and attitudes to the company as a whole will be affected. But such a situation is unstable in many senses: for example, it is all too likely that both the reputation and the reality of bad employee relations would spill over into deep distrust by consumers (and some well-known companies do indeed have that image). Of course, that is an argument that can be overstated – it is perfectly possible for a consumer's attitude to be of the form, 'This company has good customer relations but is horrible to work for'.

So, here is a strategy which structures its corporate communication around one theme, builds its corporate strategy on that theme, and bases its marketing on that theme. Underlying that strategy is the basic homework of listening, the formal research with consumers, the awareness of stakeholders' attitudes and ideas – the dialogue which is discussed in more detail in the next chapter.

Dissonance is the name which Leon Festinger gave to the concept of organizing ideas around a dominant theme.[6] People prefer consistency, and tend to assume the best about a person of whom they already think well, and to assume the worst about one of whom, albeit in some areas, they think badly or often know little. The preference for consistency means that good corporate communication pays off: the psychologist calls it dissonance-aversion; an economist might call it the multiplier; a company director could think of it as value for money.

Summary

Corporate communication is not an option. It is happening to all companies all the time, sometimes haphazardly and often without real planning. This chapter offers three reasons why corporate communication should not be left to chance:

1. Corporate communication is an indispensable part of product marketing. In the case of all products apart from that of cheap commodities, the consumer's perception of the product extends to his or her attitude towards the supplier. For the consumer the 'complete product' includes some form of relationship with the supplier.

2. Corporate strategy and corporate communications are integral parts of a single system. The best advice for a company which is thinking of 'adding-on' a corporate communication programme without reappraising its strategy is: 'Don't'.

3. An effective programme of corporate communication should be based on dialogue. A company that is a good listener can focus its programme in one area so well that the whole relationship between company and stakeholder comes to life.

References

1. William H. Davidow, *Marketing High Technology: An Insider's View* (Collier Macmillan, London, 1986).
2. I owe the phrase 'complete product' and its development in the field of high technology marketing to Davidow above.
3. Robert Heller, *The Supermarketers* (Sidgwick and Jackson, London 1987).
4. This programme for strategy formation is described in Gerry Johnson and Kevan Scholes, *Exploring Corporate Strategy* (Prentice/Hall International, London, 1984).
5. The Shell case study is given in H. Frazier Moore and Frank B. Kalupa, *Public Relations: Principles, Cases and Problems* (Richard D. Irwin Inc., Illinois, 9th ed., 1985).
6. Leon Festinger, *A Theory of Cognitive Dissonance* (Harper and Row, New York, 1957). This is discussed in Keith Williams, *Behavioural Aspects in Marketing* (Heinemann, London, 1987).

CHAPTER 2

THE CORPORATE DIALOGUE

ℭ~ℭ

Mᴀɴᴀɢᴇᴍᴇɴᴛ is an information system. It receives two kinds of information:

1. Instructions from superiors.
2. Information about the environment in which these instructions are to be interpreted.

The lower the level in the firm, the clearer the instructions become; the environment grows simpler, and the task of interpreting the environment is relatively easy. On the other hand, the higher the level in the firm, the less complete the instructions become, and interpretation becomes more complex. At the top levels in the firm, information of the first type does not exist at all, and the job consists almost entirely of creating policy out of information picked up from the environment.

That is obvious, of course, but it sets the framework for this chapter, which sees the whole corporate environment in terms of flows of communication between everyone connected with the firm. Each agent gives, receives, and interprets information and the firm as a whole exchanges information with its stakeholders. It is a many-layered, continually-changing dialogue.

It is described here under four sections:

1. Core communications.
2. Strategic communication.
3. The firm as speaker.
4. The firm as listener.

But it should not be supposed that, because the description is subdivided into four sections, the dialogue itself can be subdivided as conveniently. It is as much part of an integral system, in which the parts are as useless on their own as, say, the inner ear.

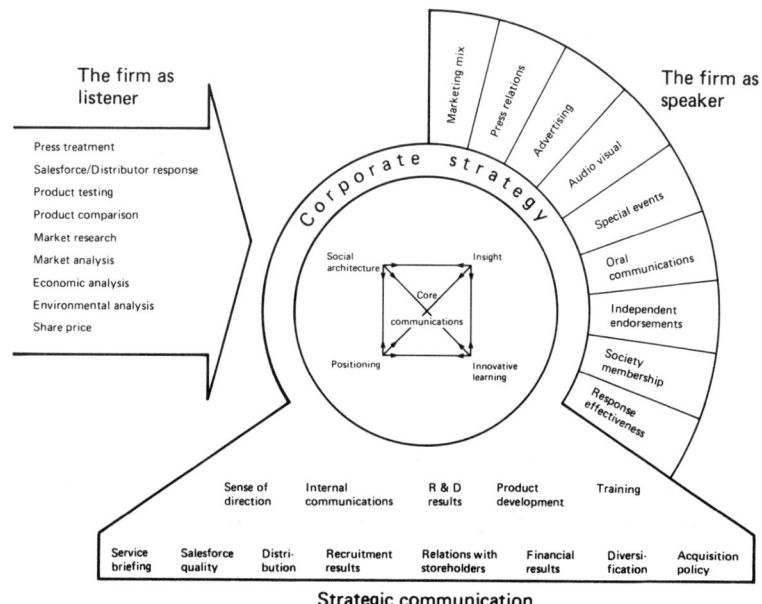

Fig. 2.1 The corporate dialogue.

The structure of the chapter is set out diagrammatically in Fig. 2.1.

Core communications

As a director of your company you receive a massive quantity of information. Leaving aside for a moment any problems of absorbing and handling it, suppose that you have perfect recall, infinite reading speeds and a hot-oven temperature IQ. How, under such ideal conditions should the information you receive be put to use? What kind of communication would now ideally flow from you? The answer is, communication appropriate to the role of leadership. In their book on leadership, *Leaders: The strategies for taking charge*, Warren Bennis and Burt Nanus have described what that means.[1]

First of all, you could communicate *vision*. 'Insight' might be a happier word, with fewer suggestions of the hero gazing into the future, but vision is in fact more accurate because it acknowledges that there are many different interpretations of the corporate environment and opportunity, all of which are equally right. The leader is able to organize the information he receives about the environment into a coherent story which others find understandable and persuasive. This is the first creative and interpretative act in the corporate dialogue.

The second is organizational design, or as Bennis and Nanus call it, *social architecture*. Over the years, an organization settles comfortably into a shape appropriate to its long-standing habits. A mature organization tends to develop a 'formalistic' structure, in which decisions are made by a combination of remote leadership and established rules; a very young or rapidly-changing organization is often dominated by one 'personality' who is a role model for everyone else in the firm. The third point in the triangle (see Fig. 2.2) is the 'collegiate' structure, which aims to reach agreement by consensus rather than compliance, and where instructions from superiors are deliberately kept weak and incomplete. Where necessary, leadership communicates change in the social architecture of an organization. This is not for change's sake, but to enable an organization, which has grown deaf to all types of communication other than the ones that it is accustomed to hear, to respond to, and in turn to communicate, a new message.

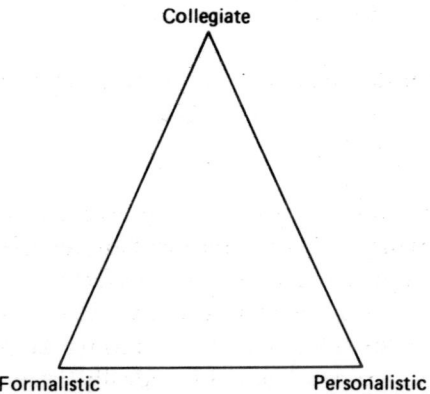

Fig. 2.2 Leadership space: three extreme types of organization.

The third feature of leadership communication is that it invites the participation of others in the essential task of *positioning* the organization accurately in the business environment. The positioning task is to ask what the main changes in the business environment will be. An airline, for example, has to consider probable changes in travelling patterns and in passengers' expectations in the future. Effective leadership communication is far better able to command commitment and trust in the strategy that is developed to meet those changes if senior management has been involved in working out what the changes are likely to be, and how the company should respond to them. The alternative would be an imposed strategy, based on assumptions which the management might well find to be implausible – and if this imposed method is adopted, the whole initiative of change and of communicating that change risks being eroded by lack of trust and commitment from the start.

If positioning requires that the company's leadership should be receptive to the views and participation of other senior managers, the fourth feature of leadership communication, *innovative learning*, focuses specifically on open-mindedness, learning from mistakes and listening to the contributions of colleagues. This is the opposite of the stereotype of the corporation man, who seeks a company ethos to admire and emulate, and who competes with his colleagues in uncritical acceptance of it. The shift towards openness and humaneness in management, willingness to acknowledge mistakes, listen to subordinates, to consider apparently wild ideas, to co-operate and to see the funny side, occurred most evidently during the 1960s, with the publication of a flood of studies on the inefficiencies of rigid organizational structures compared with open ones.[2] There were some chief executives, however, who understood this long before it became popular wisdom. The following is one of many illustrations of this openness in practice:

> A prominent junior executive of IBM was involved in a risky venture for the company, and managed to lose over $10 million in a gamble. It was a disaster. When Watson (IBM's founder) called the nervous executive into his office, the young man blurted out, 'I guess you want my resignation?' Watson said, 'You can't be serious. We've just spent $10 million educating you!'[3]

Vision, social architecture, positioning and learning – these are the four dimensions of 'core communications', the central process of formulating corporate strategy, round which the whole of a company's operation and communications programme is organized. Given leadership of this standard, the corporate communication programme will be able to speak within a clear frame of reference, expressing a well-defined objective. In the absence of that decisive start-point, the problem of knowing what to say is a symptom of the underlying loss of strategic direction in the firm.

But to conclude this section on a positive note, let us assume that the company's core communications are properly in place, and that the company does indeed have a well-defined corporate strategy to communicate. We shall now follow through the corporate dialogue.

Strategic communication

Here we consider the concrete realization of the company's strategy. Each of the 13 areas of activity indicated in this section are exercises, not simply in communication, which may imply instructions and standing orders just as much as interaction between people, but in dialogue. The concept of dialogue has been explored by Carl Rogers[4], who described the growth of 'congruence' between two people, each of whom find that their *own* communications become clearer if they trust and understand the other. Once that dialogue is established, however, it becomes richer as people direct their own creative energies into it.

From that starting point, the 13 fields of strategic communication may be quickly described. Everyone connected with the firm – employees, managers and stakeholders – has a clear *sense of direction* of the firm; managers and employees in particular frequently have the opportunity to discuss it and feel that they are participating in it. As part of the same programme, the firm's *internal communications* are good; the firm avoids the little fiefdoms of secrecy which are so damaging to members' sense of responsibility and belonging. There is a choice between 'I don't know what goes on, so why should I care?' and 'I am being kept informed, so I shall participate'. Seen in this light, good communication is equivalent to recruiting responsible participation from staff.

Good *research and development* results flow directly from a well-positioned corporate strategy. Here is the clearest index of a company's success in choosing its battleground. It is now acknowledged wisdom that a firm should fight the competition on a narrow enough front to be able to dominate its market, and one of the many reasons for this strategy is that research and development results are much more likely to pay off if they are sharply focused. So, indeed, is the related field of *product development*, the period of closest partnership between all the specialist departments of the firm. Here, above all, is where a platform of good communications, having built confidence in each other's skills, is shown to be indispensable. This is neatly illustrated with the following story.

> One of the largest food-processing companies in the United Kingdom repeatedly failed in its attempt to develop a successful piecrust mix. Test market after test market proved to be a disaster. Each year the lab came up with a new recipe that would not fail and each year it did flop – literally – at least in the important test markets. Executives got so bored with the annual fizzles that they started to refer to it as Project Lazarus, since it seemed to be resurrected from the dead so many times. Now, only because the company kept at it and finally came up with a winner, this piecrust mix is its leading product both in sales and profits. [5]

The clearest opportunity to present the corporate strategy in an unambiguous and considered way is in *training and education*, which, as in the case of Stanley Tools (see Case Study 1 in Chapter 9, page 107) which has established an outstanding reputation in the United Kingdom for its success in working with young people, can become the theme which brings into focus the whole range of a company's activities. The function of company training is one of immense power and responsibility, shaping people's lives, leaving them frustrated or enabling them to grow.

Just as effective training becomes practically impossible without a sound base of good core communications, so is the function of *service briefing*, the critically important communication of the company's will to agent, supplier and to service departments within the company. Advertising agents, marketing consultants, research consultancies, component suppliers all live on a knife-edge between knowing the mind of the corporate client and being left alone to imagine what the client really means. Briefing is a specialist skill in its own right, but it depends on the existence of a properly-articulated corporate strategy.

So, too, do relations with the *sales force* and *distributors*. In both these fields, the information that a company can get back – if it is receptive to it – is invaluable and equivalent to a continuous and massive programme of market research. In its *recruitment results* and indeed in its *relations with stakeholders* as a whole, the dialogue takes place in a very literal sense; what matters to these groups, just as well as hearing a well-articulated corporate strategy, is evidence that their own problems and questions are being answered; that the company is responsive to them and can listen.

The marriage of a clear position and willingness to listen is of course equally critical in the company's policy on *diversification* and *acquisition* – will the company become merely one of the conglomerates which has lost its way? – and in the interpretation of *financial results*. A given set of rules may appear entirely different, depending on the context in which they are presented; we are not considering here the well-known skill of accentuating the positive side of pedestrian results, but of recognizing the function of the signal of the effectiveness of a company's strategy.

This set of headings illustrates the proposition made at the start of this chapter, that management is an information system. These headings (the list is not complete, but it covers the most important areas) are, in a sense, information exchanges, in which the company interacts with its stakeholders. This is not simply a 'corporate communication programme', rather, it is part of the corporate strategy itself.

The firm as speaker

However, the dialogue has to be extended. The firm possesses a range of tools available for use in the task of communicating with its stakeholders in competition with many other conflicting messages which target groups receive almost continually. We begin here with a brief look at the 'marketing mix'. It is impossible to make clear distinction between product marketing and corporate communi-cations, because consumers wish to purchase a 'complete product', a concept which includes confidence in the supplier as well as in the product itself, and because a firm is, essentially, defined by its products. Certainly, it is normally true that a company produces far more information about itself through the medium of its products than it does in any other way.

Through the *marketing mix*, the firm speaks to its stakeholders in a huge number of ways. The following are just some of them: product range, product quality, distribution, stock levels, dealer support, pricing, discounts, credit, packaging, samples, exhibitions, selling methods, sales aids, point of sale display, advertising, sales promotion, and after sales service.[6]

As a result of this effort, the company will have gone a long way down the road towards defining itself to its stakeholders, but there are still many extremely useful communication tools waiting to be deployed, such as press relations, which should perhaps more accurately be described as *media relations* (see Chapter 5), since this includes radio and television as well as the national and local press. The reader of this book should by now be familiar with the rich range of opportunities for working with the press, from news and feature stories in the national press, to product support in the trade and consumer press, also through participating in a two-way flow of information to and from the media.

Advertising normally takes the form of product advertising except in the common case of firms in which the difference between the company and the brand is almost or entirely non-existent – the case of hotel chains, oil companies, insurance companies and airlines, for instance. This can be backed by audio-visual media, which includes a now rapidly expanding range of opportunities, from traditional film and video to the electronic floppy disk direct interaction with clients through Prestel and personal computers.

Special events (see also page 89) provide the company with a marvellous opportunity to have fun. Is that appropriate for a company with serious intentions? Indeed it is – a sense of enjoyment is one of the recurring themes of good leadership and of a firm whose management works well together; the outrageous metaphor is a well-known step in the process of scientific discovery – Friedrich von Kekulé, who discovered the ring-like structure of organic compounds, saw it in terms of whirling serpents biting their own tails – and the use of games, with their serious and non-serious content, is one of the most important of all methods of improving the technology of information and the techniques of management.

With the special events, or the art of making things happen, firms are constrained only by the limits of their imagination and budget.

Oral communications cover the range of speeches, round-table discussions, telephone contact, and the endorsement of dependent third parties – such as distributors – acting on behalf of the company. *Independent endorsement* can be both a target and a leading signal of the success of a communications programme, when a company is recommended or quoted by people who do not have a direct stake in it. *Society membership* refers to the participation of a company in its trade society and in its industry. It can be a chore to participate in the committees of an industry association, and there is a temptation to act as a 'free rider' – relying on the association doing its job to maintain the good name of the industry, without taking the trouble to participate in its work. It would be nice, in a moralistic sense, to warn that such behaviour serves a company ill in the end, but there are indeed some go-it-alone companies which cast that in doubt. On the other hand, the role of companies as agents of social reform and charity sponsors has done much to change public attitudes to companies in recent years – as well as to change companies' perceptions of their own responsibilities. For example see the Shell/Livewire (page 21) and the TSB (page 79) case studies.

Finally, *response effectiveness* refers to the company that is open to comment and criticism from outside. It is the opposite end of the spectrum from bureaucracy, where the shutters come down against criticism and new ideas, and the company is reduced to repeating a stock response, hiding behind the corporate ramparts for fear that some of the critical barbs will sting.

That is no more than a brief round up of some of the communication tools available for a company. In a sense it is like an instrument panel – the opportunities for getting things done are enormous, but if the switches are not pulled in a co-ordinated manner, the pilot could be in for a crash. Yet much can be done by a firm acting on its own – indeed, the really heavy work is that of developing the core communications and the strategic communications in the first place; after that is done, a focus and a programme are indeed, *de facto* already in place, and the switches of communication can be pulled with rich results.

The firm as listener

The first channel of information available to the firm is free. Most companies, apart from the smallest, have a systematic method of monitoring *press treatment*. The monitoring itself can be expensive, since it can extend to press cuttings delivered on the morning of the publication, and full transcripts of broadcasts, but the many firms which do not use this abundant source of information to the full bear a heavy opportunity cost. One problem is too much information and the last thing a director wants on his desk is a mass of press cuttings. The task of condensing press comment into a summary which is brief, yet contains the critical information is one that few firms have achieved satisfactorily.

The second source of abundant information is *salesforce/distributor response*. This is perhaps the most important guide of all in the task of developing a product in the market place. Product testing and product comparisons are usually a systematically exploited information medium for marketing departments and in fact form part of the massive area of *market research* (see Chapter 3). The scope of current market research techniques is so large that many firms find that they do not use it fully – it is hard to know where to begin, and there are abundant stories of mis-specified market research producing misleading answers – and being believed. Nonetheless, it represents probably the most important of all methods of information gathering open to a firm.

Market analysis and *economic analysis* are essentially another way of referring to desk research. Economic analysis is usually accompanied by techniques such as forecasting, which should never be believed, but which, if well done, force management to open its mind to a much wider range of possible futures. *Environmental analysis* broadens the frame of reference into a study of society, its anxieties, and the possible long-term secular developments which a firm must take into account in its planning.

Finally, a further instance of free information, the firm's share price is full of significance about where the firm actually stands in relation to all its marketplaces – the markets for products, equities, corporate takeovers and even recruitment. Yet the share price is scarcely 'pure' and a firm can do less or more to explain to financial analysts where it stands and what it is planning to do. Indeed this brings us full circle again to our theme of dialogue. With each of the information media we have just listed, the firm is both listener and speaker; it is part of a pattern of communication given and received.

Summary

Management is an information system and all strategic action taken by the firm can be seen as some form of interpretation of information. At higher levels in the firm, the task of interpretation is much larger and more difficult because at that level, the firm has to develop its own strategy, and cannot just interpret what has been prescribed for it. This process of development is described under 'core communication' (above). The dialogue that flows from this first stage of corporate strategy formulation has been described under 'strategic communication', and a checklist of 'information exchanges' covering the essential strategic activities of the firm provided. Under 'the firm as speaker' there is a short list of the communications media available and under 'the firm as listener' the main sources of information are described.

In conclusion, all the information sources are deeply coloured by the firm's own contribution. The marketplace is a different environment precisely because the firm is an actor in it. How to fit into that environment, how to learn from it and how to communicate with it, are the business of the firm, and interaction is what we have been exploring under the theme of corporate dialogue.

References

1. Warren Bennis and Burt Nanus, *Leaders: The strategies for taking charge* (Harper & Row, New York, 1985).
2. For example, Douglas McGregor, *The Human Side of Enterprise* (McGraw Hill, New York, 1960); J.A.C. Brown, *The Social Psychology of Industry* (Penguin, 1954).
3. Bennis and Nanus, page 76.
4. Carl R. Rogers, 'A tentative formulation of a general law of interpersonal relationships' in *On Becoming a Person* (Houghton Miller, Boston, 1961).
5. Bennis and Nanus page 53.
6. These are comprehensively discussed in Malcolm McDonald, *Marketing Plans: How to prepare them, how to use them* (Heinemann, London, 1984).

Case Study
HELPING YOUNG PEOPLE – LIVEWIRE

Shell UK Ltd

Consultancy
PR Consultants Scotland.

Date
1982 pilot; 1985 project.

Summary
Shell UK retained PR Consultants Scotland to promote their 'Livewire' scheme, designed to encourage and help young people aged 16–25 to consider self-employment as a viable option.

Opportunity
The Small Business Unit of Shell UK, working with PR Consultants Scotland, had identified an opportunity to help young people who might otherwise not consider self-employment. The Livewire formula assigned each entrant interested in self-employment to an experienced individual advisor who would assist, encourage and support the youngster in their business scheme, to get them off the ground. An initial pilot scheme in Strathclyde had already demonstrated that the formula was effective. The opportunity therefore existed to develop 'Livewire' into a national scheme, which would benefit both the young people involved and Shell UK.

Strategy

1. To develop an awareness of the scheme amongst young people in the appropriate age group, in an effort to maximize entries.
2. To overcome an important credibility gap by conveying the message to young people that self-employment is a realistic option whatever their age, experience or background.
3. To develop an awareness of 'Livewire' among other relevant groups in order to attract support for the scheme in terms of local sponsorship, volunteer advisors, etc.

Programme
PR Consultants Scotland initiated an intensive media campaign for the 'Livewire' scheme, commencing in 1985. This campaign was implemented both nationally and through the regional network of 'Livewire', to give local emphasis. The campaign included the following:

1. The issuing of PR and promotional guidelines to all 'Livewire' regional offices.
2. The provision of a hotline for regional office queries to be answered.
3. A national launch function for the media.
4. The provision of information packs individualized to each regional 'Livewire' office, for use with local media and other organizations.
5. The release of localized information packs to media throughout the United Kingdom at regular intervals.
6. The release of a radio tape interview with the Chairman of Shell UK about 'Livewire', giving local contact details for each region.
7. A massive mailing campaign to all relevant establishments, from youth clubs and community centres to libraries and enterprise agencies.
8. The release of regular updates to regional media.
9. Liaison with national media including television and magazines, to produce feature articles.
10. Advertising on local travel networks.

11. The loan of portable displays on 'Livewire' to banks, local organizations, etc.
12. The issuing of a 'Livewire' newsletter.

Results

1. Widespread media coverage (710 editorial items, including 12 television and 56 radio) which generated 33 percent of all entries, and brought in additional sponsorship money and advisors offering help.
2. An increase in young people's confidence in being self-employed, through the publicity and information given out.
3. Entries from 3,500 young people interested in working for themselves – from past experience this would indicate around 15-30 per cent went on to become their own bosses.
4. Interest was created at an international level, with other countries expressing an interest in establishing similar schemes.
5. Shell UK committed themselves to operating an annual 'Livewire' scheme for a further five years.

CHAPTER 3

GRASPING THE
MARKET RESEARCH NETTLE

ℰ✇ℯ

What market research can tell you

There are two ways of getting the information needed for planning a communications programme. The first is by the direct experience of selling and operating in a market; the second is by a programme of market research. Of these, the first is continuously being renewed, and is free; however, it is liable to misinterpretation, and is often haphazard; it is retrospective, giving information about past actions, rather than proposed ones, and in the case of new initiatives, it is not available at all. The second, effective market research, can be more reliable. It can be made directly relevant to future plans, and it is accessible to every company (provided they have the necessary budget and will).

It is important to remember, however, that some market research can be shallow, uninformed and downright misleading. Frequently companies are encouraged to indulge in what are called 'market research projects' in order to get cheap publicity when the results of such studies are released. Frequently, too, such exercises can backfire on the sponsoring organization and on the promoters. It is sad but true that on many occasions information sought from a member of the public in the name of research is not what it seems! Moves taken by the Market Research Society to ensure that researchers show credentials so that the genuine researcher can be identified are to be welcomed. The Market Research Society has an important role in this area and it is best to deal only with member organizations which work to their accepted standards. Details of the society appear in Appendix 2 on page 131.

The following is just some of the information that market research can provide:

The size of the market

Research can show:

1. The actual size of the market, both for home sales and for exports.
2. The potential size of the market, for both existing and new products.
3. The potential size of the market given certain conditions such as a new product launch, a new programme of marketing and corporate communication, both by one's own company and by others.
4. A company's probable sales over a period, given a certain level of expenditure on corporate communications and promotion.

Potential customers

In the case of consumer products, a company can use market research to develop a profile of their actual or potential customers – their income, socio-economic group and location.

   In the case of industrial companies, it can produce a very detailed picture of customers – which kinds of firms, and which individuals in firms make the purchasing decisions.

Needs and attitudes

Without attitude surveys, a corporate communications programme is flying blind: a good illustration of the crucial importance of testing a corporate communications programme as it proceeds is the background of market research against which Shell carried out its consumer relations campaign described in Chapter 1 (page 7). This use of market research spills over into the strategically central area of product design and development – and here we should not take the word 'product' too literally since (as we noted in Chapter 1) the concept of the 'complete product' implies that from a consumer's point of view the quality and reputation of the company may be every bit as important, and indeed impossible to distinguish from, the specification of the product.

Problem diagnosis

Market research is the essential diagnostic method for companies faced with a problem such as declining sales, market share or profitability. It allows problems of poor salesforce performance or poor promotion to be distinguished from those of, say, the emergence of a relative disadvantage in the face of a major new corporate communications initiative by a competitor.

It is hard to overstate the importance of market research as the prime source of strategic information for the company. Yet all too often companies try to get by without it. This is often claimed to be a method of economizing. Perhaps the real reason is that, without market research specialists on the staff, it is not always clear where to begin.

Begin by setting objectives.

Setting objectives

The most important part of a market research programme is the bit that you do before asking questions of anyone but yourself. What is your company trying to say? How would it like to be seen? What assumptions does it make, or would it like to be able to make, about its target audience's attitudes? The answers to these questions must come, in the first instance, from you. After discussion, these become the hypotheses that are tested by the market research, which is organized round a clearly-stated programme.

For example, a hotel chain may propose to develop a programme of corporate communications in the light of evidence that it was getting less bookings than its competitors in the off-peak winter season. There are many possible reasons for this, and among them might be the hypothesis that the more serious and classical winter entertainments offered by competitors were preferred to the more 'popular' entertainments offered by one's own company. This hypothesis will then need to be tested, but not immediately by formal market research. It would need to be discussed with colleagues and managers and informal research would be done by observing what competitors did and noting comments in the trade press. In this way an iterative process is set up, in the course of which the hypothesis is refined and becomes more detailed, so that when the market research operation itself is launched, the company knows exactly what it is looking for, and has developed draft contingency plans to be carried out in case the hypothesis is confirmed or rejected. The alternative can be an expensive heartbreak; when the research comes back it yields results which either have not been guessed at or are ambiguous, and the company's response can only be 'Oh, in that case, what we *should* have asked, was . . .'

In the light of a clear statement of hypotheses and objectives, a second difficult market research issue is likely to fall into place: the budget. How valuable will the correct programme, based on accurate information, be to the company? And what will the opportunity cost be if it fails? The answers to these questions are a quite reliable guide to the value of the information, and the amount which it would be justifiable to budget for the research.

Types of research

Desk research

Of all the types of market research information available in the field of corporate communication, the largest source of data by far is that contained in existing sources. A lot of money is spent unnecessarily in rediscovering information which already exists. There are three reasons why this information is not used as much as it could be:

1. Knowing where to look can be a substantial skill in its own right. It is not usually a good use of time for a person who is not already familiar with the sources to research a single project, since the majority of the time spent will involve leafing through the wrong publications, and visiting the wrong library on the way.
2. Paying outside consultants to do this work can seem very expensive; all you are getting is information that already exists, yet you are paying hourly rates appropriate to qualified marketing consultants and economists. In fact, this is likely to be a very good use for research funds, but it seems at first sight to be more justifiable to spend that money on 'original' research – even though that research has been done many times before by other companies.
3. Much market research is confidential to the company that pays for it, and by the time it is written up as a case study, it is out of date and the moment for action has passed. Yet the problem of confidentiality is not conclusive, and there are many ways in which such information can be obtained with the consent of the company concerned. For example, it is often possible to arrange for all the companies in an industry to reveal information which can be published as a study by their trade association.

Good desk research can yield information on all aspects of the market, its size, growth, structure and changing character; on consumers' attitudes and the lessons of similar situations in export markets. In the right hands, it can yield models of the market, in which the main factors affecting consumers' responses are modelled and given their respective weights in a multiple regression programme.

In short, desk research is the essential homework that has to be done before the more glamorous, and more easily delegated, original market research programme is put into effect. Our society is glutted with good information about itself, and we really should think twice before sending researchers out there to add to this information mountain.

Face-to-face interviewing

Where the information required is complex, where it involves something which has to be seen or demonstrated, or where the people whose opinions are sought can be specifically named, it is worth setting up a programme which involves visits to homes and places of work. Other instances are surveys in which it is felt that the security of the home environment is an advantage, or where the interviewing can sensibly be done in the street or at a shopping centre.

The main disadvantage of this method is that it can be very expensive, involving travelling time and appointments. In many cases it is only possible to carry out the interview in the evenings, so that one interviewer may be limited to ten or fewer interviews in a week.

Telephone interviewing

Most market research is now carried out by means of telephone calls. It has the advantages of simplicity, safety, speed and cost. In the case of corporate image research it presents itself as a natural method, since the question itself is often a fairly simple one, which does not warrant much probing.

A company can make good use of the neatness of the telephone approach by using it as a regular survey; samples of opinion on a company and its competitors can be taken, say, annually or more often, so that trends can be revealed, and changes in attitude may be associated with specific events, such as one's own or one's competitors corporate advertising campaigns.

Omnibus surveys

One cost-effective way of showing changes in attitudes towards a company is to use an omnibus survey. As the name suggests, they are going there anyway, and you can take a ride as you wish – by 'buying a question' about your company in the survey. The right time to make the decision to do so is *before* the corporate communications programme is set up, so that attitudes towards the company at that time can be used as a benchmark against which to measure changes in the future.

Group discussions

These are expensive, but they can be extremely valuable as a means of understanding consumers' responses to advertising and ideas for future action in corporate communication, as well as their responses to products, corporate designs, literature and promotions. They are expensive because of the logistics involved: people have to be found who are both representative of the population which is being researched and who are willing to spend part of a day in discussion with strangers about a subject which is not normally their main area of interest. Indeed the greatest drawback of this method of research is that many of the people whose opinion would be most valuable (often the busiest) cannot be persuaded to come whatever the incentive.

A further problem associated with groups is that there is a risk that one group is dominated by a powerful personality who influences what the others think. So it is almost always necessary to have a series of such discussions rather than just one, and the market research consultant's task of writing up is a skilled one.

Despite these problems, group discussions are a very valuable form of market research, and they come closest to the idea of the 'corporate dialogue'. You come close to understanding what they believe, and what the real concerns are of the people amongst whom your corporate communications programme is to be launched.

Hall tests and clinics

For the sake of completeness, we should mention hall tests and clinics, in which potential customers are brought together to test products and to taste food. This is a standard method of product research.

Can you trust it?

If, at the end of the market research programme, you are sceptical about the results, then it will have proved to be an almost complete waste of money and time. There are two ways in which doubt may arise. Unless you include every member of the population in the test, then you cannot be quite sure that you have a true result, so samples have to be used, and the results are given as true within certain limits. Typically, market researchers look for a 95 per cent probability of their estimate being correct to plus-or-minus a certain percentage of their quoted figure. The details of this calculation are set out in every textbook on market research, but for the non-specialist the critically important point to remember is that, so long as the sample is a truly random one, the accuracy of the result does not depend on the size of the whole population, but on the size of the sample that has been surveyed.

A much greater source of potential error lies in the design of the questionnaire, and indeed the logical integrity of the survey in the first place. The problem is that many questions are just too complex to survey at reasonable cost. For example, one question in public debate, which an importer might wish to survey as part of a corporate communications programme, is whether the United Kingdom should import corned beef from Ethiopia. For most people the immediate reaction is likely to be 'No, Ethiopians are starving and their country needs all the food it produces.' A second reaction might be, 'But they need the foreign exchange with which to buy grain and vital agricultural equipment. If we don't import the corned beef, it will rot and the country will suffer even more.' A more considered reaction still might be, 'But they shouldn't have been producing beef in the first place. How many peasants had to vacate the land for the beef herds?'

In the end, there is nothing for it but to recognize that the question is so complex that there is almost no market research response that makes sense. Here is a recipe for the opinion war, 'Research shows that people approve of our action in providing a needed market for Ethiopian beef,' one report might read. But equally 'valid' research could show that 'consumers approve our action in boycotting Ethiopian beef sales, and thereby helping the peasant-subsistence farmers.'

That does not mean that all market research issues, to be really trustworthy, have to be really simple. But it does mean that a company which organizes its market research cleverly can comfort itself with exactly the reassuring results that it is looking for. Anton Chekov's plays and short stories are recognized as brilliant not least because they portray problems 'with no beginning and no end and no solution'; this is the level of complexity of the world in which corporate communication has to operate. The process of simplification in such a world becomes either a process of clarification, or a process of fixing the results. Needless to say, there are no simple rules on how to distinguish between the two.

Summary

Market research is really another way of saying 'information-gathering', and as such it provides the essential link that distinguishes the corporate communication fantasy from the genuine dialogue which places the company in its market.

Effective market research must be based on a clear statement of objectives and of hypotheses to be tested. In the light of this framework for the research, the choice of research method should be made, and almost always this involves a combination of methods, of which desk research should be the first part. Essential though it is, market research can produce wild results; this is not because of the statistical problems of sampling, but because of the logical problems of reducing a complex issue to simple questions.

This chapter has produced some guidelines for grasping the market research nettle (and lists some further reading below); but much the most important guideline can be stated as follows: first of all, think the problem through; market research can never be a substitute for that. It can be an expensive means of confirming error; or the essential source of data for an effective programme of corporate communications.

Further reading

1. Paul N. Hague and Peter Jackson, *Do Your Own Market Research*, Kogan Page, 1987. This is an excellent and extremely practical book for anyone involved in the practice of market research. It is clearly written and well signposted. Highly recommended.
2. David A. Aaker and George S. Day, *Marketing Research*, John Wiley, 1986. A very comprehensive textbook, complete with cases.
3. Sunny Crouch, *Marketing Research for Managers*, Heinemann. Useful background reading.
4. F. Stewart DeBruicker and David J. Reibstein, *Cases in Marketing Research*. This is chiefly designed for teaching purposes, but it is very valuable as an antidote to the books which make market research sound simple. The complexities described in the last section of this chapter are abundantly illustrated in this book.

CHAPTER 4

CHOOSING AND USING
A CONSULTANCY

℮≈℮

CHOOSING and using corporate communications specialists is a process which strikes fear into the hearts of many executives. While most companies are likely to have used an advertising agency before, relatively few may have used the services of a public relations consultancy or even direct marketing specialists. Yet when such specialists are properly chosen, the benefits to a company of whatever size can be considerable. In the same way that you would not tackle legal or financial matters without specialist advisors, so it makes sense not to attempt to improve corporate communications without help.

Types of consultancy

The three main types of advisors are advertising agencies, public relations consultancies and direct marketing suppliers.

Advertising agencies have been around for well over a century and developed largely in response to the emergence of mass circulation newspapers and magazines. At their simplest, agencies were just that – they acted as agents for advertisers in taking space in the media. Because the agencies were able to raise advertising revenue for journals, they were given a discount on the advertising space booked. Since the advertiser paid the full price for the advertisement space, it was this commission which gave advertising agencies their income.

The growth of advertising this century in response to rising living standards and more sophisticated consumer tastes means that advertisers now spend over £5 billion a year on advertising in the United Kingdom. Such growth has enabled companies such as Saatchi & Saatchi to expand from a relatively small agency in the early 1970s to become a major global communications operation, spanning not only advertising but also management consultancy.

Public relations consultancies differ in one crucial respect from advertising agencies. Public relations advisors in their purest form are meant to offer companies and organizations communication help as consultants rather than agents. In theory this should mean that consultants do nothing else but offer advice. In reality, they also usually implement the communications advice they give and charge for this accordingly.

Although in-house public relations departments have been found in many companies for decades, it has only been in the 1980s that consultancies have come into their own and have been growing at an annual rate of at least 25 per cent in terms of the amount spent by companies. Some 45 out of the top 50 British companies now employ a specialist public relations consultancy.

Direct marketing is still in its relative infancy in the United Kingdom although it is one of the fastest growing marketing services sectors. The largest component of direct marketing is direct mail, but the sector also covers such techniques as direct response advertisements and telephone marketing. As a communications method it is likely to grow in popularity and effectiveness in the 1990s.

The communications mix – how to decide

The first stage in deciding what sort of communications help you need is to carry out an audit of just who you are trying to reach and why. Such communications audits are growing in popularity amongst companies since it forces them to sit back and think exactly who they are trying to influence.

An audit can be carried out in several levels – from the basic 'brainstorming' sessions between executives themselves to employing a consultancy to carry out a full-scale audit. The processes involved, however, are the same. Initially, the company's objectives should be identified – is the aim of the communications programme simply to increase sales? Or are you trying to re-position your products and want to inform consumers? What do the various target groups you are concerned with think about your company? How is your image put across, from such basics as the way in which the switchboard answers telephone calls to the logo on shops or fleet vehicles? What do groups such as the media and your employees think about the company and its performance?

Armed with all these comments, the next step is to assess them in the light of your objectives and develop a strategy to influence the target groups. It is here that you have to decide whether to use advertising, sponsorship, public relations, direct marketing or other techniques.

Implementing the strategy – hints on choosing advisors

1. It is important that you get to know your potential advisors as well as possible before employing them. Therefore, keep your shortlist as small as possible – three or four – rather than the usual half dozen or more.
2. When drawing up a shortlist, establish something about the company's track-record. Ask them how often they keep clients on average. (Some advisors have a habit of winning accounts and losing them a few months later.) Ask for the names and numbers of clients who have left and telephone them to find out why.
3. Establish clearly who is going to be working on your account once you have given them the business. Many communications companies put forward their smoothest, most experienced staff when a new business prospect is involved. You may not get the same calibre of people actually working for you.
4. Personal chemistry is important. If the advisor is to become an extension of your company in the outside world, it is essential to get on with the individuals involved. Surprisingly, not all of them are good at inter-personal skills.
5. While budgeting is important, don't be mean when dealing with advisors. Companies that will spend £5 million on an advertising campaign, will baulk at spending £50,000 on a public relations programme, or even £5,000 on a direct mailshot. With PR consultancies especially, it is the time you are paying for – so the less you pay the less you will get.
6. Remember that your advisors are professional people whom you are paying to carry out specialist tasks. Treat them as you would the company lawyers or accountants, i.e. with respect and not as odd-jobbers to carry out unimportant tasks for you.

(Further hints on choosing PR consultants may be found in Chapter 8, page 93 and Appendix 1 on page 118.)

Public relations consultancies

Why choose a PR consultancy? Perhaps one of the most important reasons for choosing a consultancy is that they can often be a more effective, both in terms of cost and achievement, means of communication than other techniques. Consultancies can refine the target market down to the groups you want to influence most – an approach called 'narrowcasting'.

It is hardly surprising, therefore, that PR has picked up some of the money previously spent on advertising. But it has also had to prove its effectiveness as a communications medium. PR consultancies are now far more aware of the need to measure the effectiveness of their strategies, through such means as market research, and this discipline has enabled them to prove their own worth as against other means of communication.

Public relations activity in the United Kingdom in the 1980s has also received a boost from the growth in media opportunities available, typified by the addition of a new television channel, two morning breakfast television programmes, and new newspapers such as *The Independent*. This fragmentation of the media gives PR consultancies more opportunity to get their message across to a specialist audience.

Increasingly companies have turned to PR specialists to help cope with problems such as redundancies or factory closures, and to deal not only with the media but also with other groups such as employees. At the same time, new areas of activity have emerged, such as the growth in financial services. In the mid-1980s, moreover, PR specialists were very much in evidence as advisors to companies involved in the various mega takeover battles.

Companies that want to develop a PR programme would appear to have two clear options: they can create or enhance an internal public relations department or they can employ an outside consultancy. In practice, however, companies also have a third option: they can combine the two to get the best of both worlds.

In-house PR departments

Many companies have built up some type of public relations function over the years, often starting out as an adjunct to the marketing department and then being established in its own right. In-house public relations departments have a number of advantages over consultancies, but also some drawbacks. The main advantage of in-house PR is simply that the department's activities are geared full-time towards the company concerned. A consultancy, on the other hand, will have a number of clients and will only be able to apportion a part of its time according to the agreed fee.

If the in-house PR department has the support of the managing director and other key executives (and all PR needs such support to be of any use) then internal PR is in a better position to reflect accurately the needs of the organization to the external world. Such internal departments are particularly useful if the company is involved in high profile activities. It is vital in these cases for the internal PR department to present an accurate picture of what is happening within the company – be it a strike or a takeover bid – in response to inquiries from the media.

Yet, there are drawbacks to an in-house PR department. For example, it could be that the department is too dominated by the marketing function, and press releases simply become 'puffs' and house journals are nothing more than sales catalogues. Moreover, the in-house department may be asked to do too much, simply because many members of senior management are unclear exactly what is required from the department. Conversely, since a consultancy is charging for its time, senior executives should have a clearer idea exactly what is being done for them. Internal PR departments may also suffer from a lack of specialist knowledge about different types of PR and the media. It is unfair to expect the typical in-house PR department to be proficient in every area, such as corporate and financial PR, parliamentary liaison, house journal production, and so on. This, however, is where the specialist PR consultancy can come into its own.

Advantages of using external consultancies

A consultancy has access to a wider range of experience, talents, contacts, and expertise than an in-house department. Executives are usually of a higher calibre for a lower cost, since overheads are shared among a number of the consultancy's clients. Other advantages include the ability to handle special projects and peak loads, and to vary a PR programme according to client and market demands. Consultancy staff are drawn from a variety of sources: journalism, marketing, law, education, industrial psychology, finance, industrial relations, market research, broadcasting, industry, and research. While many specialize in certain fields and others undertake a broad range of activities, the one basic skill that is supposed to be common to all is their ability to communicate effectively.

What exactly do consultancies do to earn their fees? They offer everything from detailed analysis of an organization's communications requirements, through advice on all levels, to the planning and implementation of communications programmes. They liaise with the media, offer sales force support, event management, crisis planning, lobbying and direct communications – such as receptions, seminars, and exhibitions.

Media relations are probably the backbone of most PR communications campaigns. Consultancies are paid to know exactly which journals, writers and broadcasters will be interested in particular items of information. They know how these people actually work and what their needs are. Consultancies can also offer journalists and others off-the-record briefings, analyse media comment for their clients, and gather market information; all as part of a well-managed media relations programme.

When choosing a consultancy it is important to bear in mind that some consultancies are more specialist in certain areas. For example, some consultancies specialize in lobbying and parliamentary work, while others are strong in corporate or consumer affairs. It will soon become clear from the type of clients and work carried out just what category a particular consultancy falls into. Some consultancies, of course, will claim to offer a 'full-service' – providing all the communications functions. While some do have the resources for this, most do not. A further question to consider is whether you want to deal with a small or large consultancy. A large consultancy may have more resources and expertise to handle your business. On the other hand, a small consultancy may feel more committed to making a success of your communications. There is no right answer about small or large; much simply depends on how well you get on with them at the early stages.

Pitching for your business

What happens when a consultancy is asked to pitch for your business? As with the advertising world, PR consultancies will offer a two-stage approach. First is the credentials pitch, which is aimed at showing you just what sort of consultancy they are and what they have done for other clients. A good consultancy will also take the opportunity to question you more closely about your company and communication aims. The second stage is for the consultancy to come up with some ideas about how to achieve your communications objectives. Do not, however, expect this pitch to be too detailed unless you are prepared to pay for the consultancy's time involved. (Most pitches are unpaid.)

If you ask a consultancy to spend time and creative effort coming up with a good PR programme for nothing, then the money has to be recouped from somewhere. That somewhere is the consultancy's existing clients who are effectively getting a poorer service to enable the consultancy to come up with bright ideas for you for nothing. So if you employ this consultancy, they will be doing the same to you when pitching for other companies' business.

When you have decided to employ a consultancy, it is important to agree the fees in advance. There are a variety of systems used by consultancies, ranging from a fixed fee payable monthly to carry out a specified programme, to a total time-based system depending on how much time it takes the consultancy to achieve your communications needs. Most consultancies use a mixture of both; a basic fee plus payment for hours worked. Remember, however, that if you pay your consultancy too little, they will be less effective for you in the long run. (See also Chapter 8.)

Getting value from your communications advisors

The simple truth is that you will only get as much value out of your advisors as the amount of time, effort, and resources that you are prepared to put in. If your corporate culture is against divulging information to outsiders (you don't like joining trade associations, for example) then you are going to find it difficult to open up with your communications consultants. Similarly, if you fail to give them a high priority in your internal dealings – failing, for example, to respond to telephone calls until a day or two later – then that attitude will rub off on both sides and the professional relationship will invariably end. Consultancies must, if they are to give you value, become a natural extension of your company, able to understand and work with your corporate culture.

The type of consultancy you want, therefore, and which is likely to give you the best value is one which sees its role and ambitions as being part of yours. One of the problems generated by the number of consultancies going public in recent years, has sometimes been the fact that they have generated more attention about themselves than they ever do for their clients.

A key step in getting good value from your consultancy is to identify exactly what it is you want them to achieve from the start and establish some forms of objective measurement. For example, you may want your consultancy to generate customer or trade leads. If so, you can build a code phrase or number into the response mechanism to identify the level of leads generated. Even if no such code is used, then you will be aware of the normal level of leads generated and therefore be able to calculate the proportion of extra leads. In such a situation, you may be able to negotiate with the consultancy to pay a lower initial fee for their work but provide a bonus on a sliding scale according to how many leads are generated. The consultancy will not usually like such a system – but it may give them the motivation they need.

Another way of ensuring value is to undertake some attitude studies before and after the consultancy has completed its communications work. For example, you can identify employee attitudes towards some aspect of your company before and after the consultancy has sought to change those attitudes.

Not surprisingly, the technique of trying for some objective measurement of a communications programme works wonders in ensuring that the consultancy pulls all the stops out! Even column inches of editorial mentions in newspapers and magazines should be used as some kind of measure. Consultancies will often argue that such mentions don't matter and that it is overall attitudes which count. What it usually means is that they have insufficient media contact to generate the desired level of editorial mentions. If such mentions don't count in the consultancy's opinion, carry out attitude surveys instead.

Keeping your consultancy on its toes requires you to delegate responsibility to a member of your staff who should maintain close liaison with the consultancy and monitor progress. If you really feel matters are going adrift, then tell the consultancy as soon as you can – don't let problems fester and multiply because they could cause irreparable harm to your corporate image rather than harm the consultancy.

But, equally, ensuring best value for money from your consultancy does not mean expecting the impossible. Establishing realistic goals is as important as ensuring that they are met. Unrealistic communications objectives – such as putting a minor change in your product on the front page of the *Financial Times* – create problems for you and your consultancy.

Summary

Those who do not already use communication specialists should not shrink from considering this option. Three main groups of advisors – advertising agencies, public relations consultancies and direct marketing suppliers – have been identified, and also the services they offer. The 'communication mix' is described and there are hints on how to choose advisors. Regarding the role of the in-house department, outside specialists can integrate with and complement its work. When using external specialists size, experience and staff competence should be considered.

In order to get value from your advisors you should understand your own attitude and that of your company in relation to communication. Being honest with yourself will pay dividends. If you (and/or your company) are secretive then it will immediately inhibit the results you are likely to get from using advisors. Value for money will relate to the amount of time, effort and resources invested in a communications project, and also the speed of reaction and action at your end of the process.

Choosing communication advisors can be a daunting task for many companies. Picking your way through the minefield of different types of advisors, however, can be best achieved by defining your communication objectives and then adopting a commonsense approach to choosing the best one for you. There is no easy technique to picking advisors – much depends on personal chemistry and their degree of commitment to you.

The company must have clear objectives and targets for an overall programme or specific campaign, and the responsibility for this rests initially within the organization itself, not with the specialist advisors. Realism in relation to the practical achievement of goals is advocated and the need for understanding and monitoring developments resulting from the PR programme.

CHAPTER 5

MEDIA RELATIONS

❦

COMMUNICATION with the media is potentially one of the most effective ways of getting your corporate message across. Television and radio, newspapers and magazines all reach the target groups you need to get in touch with. We all absorb much of our day-to-day knowledge, and base our decisions, largely on the information received from the media in all its shapes and forms.

Given its importance in the communication process, therefore, it is surprising that many business executives give so low a priority to communicating through the media and are so bad at achieving effective media relations. In many cases this is perhaps due to the poor image of the media itself: an image of hardened hacks anxious to uncover whatever 'dirt' is available and, if not, to make it up instead. Obviously, such a breed of reporters do exist. But like any extreme image, they make up only a small minority of media people.

Most journalists are like any other group of human beings. They have the same goals and aspirations, the same desire to lead a happy life, the same willingness on the whole to live and let live. There is a 'normal distribution' of all types of personalities within the media – as there is in your own company. And like most of your employees they are out to do a job of work as honestly as they can.

Yet it is important to remember that the objectives of the media are not necessarily the same as those of your company. Journalists, be they radio, television, or press, are interested in providing information for their readers, listeners, or viewers. Such information, of course, may be exactly what you want to communicate. Often, however, it may be information which you would rather was not aired in public. A new product launch, for example, is something that you clearly want publicity for. But the premature announcement of a factory closure is news that you would prefer did not get out. It is important to bear this in mind when dealing with the media. They are there to act as a channel of communication between you and your target groups; they are not there simply to repeat what you want to say.

Having said that, there are plenty of occasions when your objectives and those of the media will coincide. When you want to tell shareholders about your financial performance, for example, the media is an ideal way of imparting this information. Or when you have secured the contract to sell the proverbial ice-cubes to Eskimos then this is an achievement that the media will almost certainly want to boast about with you.

What is news?

A former editor of the *Daily Express* in the 1930s came up with this maxim for junior reporters: 'When dog bites man, that's no news. But when man bites dog, that's news!' News, in some journalists' opinion, could also be defined as 'information that someone, somewhere does not want to see in print'.

Realistically, however, news is information that will be of interest to readers, both in their professional and personal lives. What interests people? Ask yourself what you find interesting. Why do you read certain stories in a newspaper or recall particular items on a news broadcast? The answer is because such news items reflect something that is out of the ordinary. You would not be interested in reading that most people were still in work yesterday, or that most factories were working normally. Such information would clearly bore you – and drive the newspaper or magazine out of business. What is interesting, however, is when redundancies are announced or a boardroom power struggle takes place. Or when, for example, a company capitalizes on some new trend in the market.

How do journalists find news? There are a number of sources available. One of the most important is the Government, whose various branches generate considerable information which is of use and interest to many companies. This information generally comes in the form of a press release which, since it comes from a government body, is given more credence than most of the press releases which are sent out by public relations consultancies. Personal and telephone contacts are perhaps the other key sources of stories. A journalist's contacts keep him or her informed of developments and enable news items not only to be generated in this way but also to be presented in the most favourable way for these contacts.

Newspapers

How do newspapers work?

All newspapers, including the local and free press, have different management structures but, basically, their operations revolve around a news and features desk. These are the editors who determine what news and features are covered each day. Many newspapers have different staff for news and features although some, like the *Financial Times*, have the same staff writing both.

Since the *FT* is of particular interest to directors because it gives the broadest business and financial coverage of UK and international affairs, it may be useful to cite its workings as an example of newspaper practice. The *FT* has some 300 journalists working for it, of which about 30 are staff correspondents based abroad. (There are a further 70 correspondents overseas who are not on the staff but work mainly for the *FT*.) In the United Kingdom, there are about 100 writers for the newspaper and about 100 sub-editors. Sub-editors have the responsibility for checking the accuracy and grammar of an article as well as rewriting it to make it clearer. The remaining journalists are responsible for editing particular pages throughout the newspaper.

The *FT*, like all national newspapers, uses an interactive screen-based system. The article is keyed into the system by the writing journalist who then sends it electronically to the relevant page editor (UK news, for example). The page editor then checks the copy and passes it to the sub-editor. The sub will write a headline and ensure the article makes sense, before passing it back to the page editor. The article is then 'released' for typesetting by computer.

Copy deadlines for the inside of the newspaper generally start at 3.30 in the afternoon and then follow at hourly intervals until the last deadline for the front page at about 7 p.m. This first edition of the newspaper is the one that reaches the furthest parts of the United Kingdom (and in the *FT*'s case, the editions printed overseas). A further three editions are printed each night, the last one timed at about 2.30 in the morning.

Television and radio news and feature programmes work to a different schedule but the journalists involved work to the same type of system. These programmes tend to have an overall editor responsible for the entire content of the programme, with individual items put together by reporters, researchers, and producers.

Ten tips for dealing with journalists

There is no right or wrong way of dealing with journalists. Like most people, they all have their likes and dislikes and what works for some may not work for others. Yet there are some basic guidelines that may help you in talking and working with media people.

1. Remember where the balance of interest lies. In most cases you want to talk to the media to get your message across to target audiences, rather than allowing your competitors to get their views across. If you do not talk to the press, or are too busy, or delay ringing people back, then journalists may decide to talk to someone else rather than to you.

2. Brief the switchboard, your secretary and colleagues about dealing with the press. Nothing is more disruptive to effective media relations than an over-inquisitive switchboard or a secretary putting a block between you and a journalist.

3. Identify the time element involved. When you first speak to the journalist, find out whether or not it is really urgent for both of you to speak then. The importance of this is that you may have time to collect your thoughts. Speaking off the cuff is a skill which takes practice. If you have the opportunity to call back within 10 or 15 minutes, then do so and use the time to marshall your thoughts about the message you really want to get across.

4. Do remember the simple courtesies when talking on the telephone (even if the journalist is brusque with you!). It is your corporate image which is at stake if you treat a journalist curtly. If you are not the right person to speak to, then find out who the right person is and personally put the call through.

5. On or off the record? Everybody has different ideas about what this means. The golden rule is that if you do not want anything mentioned in print, then do not say it at all. The best kept secrets are the ones kept to yourself. What most journalists (but not all) mean by 'off the record' is that the information can be used in an article but should not be directly attributable to you or your company. It is usually information that you want to get across but not in a direct fashion. It is similar to 'background information'. The trick is to clarify what you have in mind when you say that something is off the record – spell it out rather than hope that the journalist's interpretation is the same as yours. 'On the record' means just that: the information can be directly attributed to you or your company.

6. Establish at the beginning of the interview – either by telephone or face-to-face – whether or not the interview is on or off the record. One of the unwritten rules of journalism is that unless you do this at the beginning, the journalist will assume that everything you say can be quoted directly. If you say it was 'off the record' at the end of the interview, the journalist will point out this was not the basis on which you were speaking. In reality, if you say it was 'off the record' at the end of the interview and the journalist objects, then usually some sort of compromise can be worked out. But the journalist will feel he is morally right if he refuses to allow you to claim it was off the record. The best and most effective interviews, according to many journalists, are where the conversation is all 'on the record'. If you are confident of what you have to say, you might as well go ahead and make it all 'on the record'. But make this clear at the start since it shows that you are aware of the tricks of the trade.

7. Do not believe you have a right to see an article before it is published. Most journalists hate doing this and most editors (especially on national newspapers) have a policy that copy should not be shown outside the premises. There are some sound reasons for not letting the copy be seen before publication; most importantly, because there may simply not be enough time. If you are worried about being misquoted, then it is legitimate either to say the conversation is all off the record unless you say certain parts are quotable. Or you can agree with the journalist for him to check the quotes with you before publication.

8. Make a few key points when talking to a journalist. It is better to answer in quotable quotes, along with practical examples, than to give long-winded explanations. Remember, most articles will answer the five key questions of journalism – who, what, when, where, and why – in some form. Prepare for the interview by asking yourself these questions in advance. Moreover, do not expect a journalist to have your depth of specialist knowledge. His job is to communicate what you have to say to people who almost certainly will have even less specialist knowledge.

9. Make contacts. The most effective way of talking to journalists is through personal contacts. If you do not know the journalist when you first speak, it pays to be rather more careful. But when you know the individual, you can sometimes explore the story idea in greater depth simply because you have already established some common ground between you. Making contacts, of course, is not necessarily easy. But the effort pays off in the end.

10. What happens when things go wrong? Mistakes happen, and to you they always seem like the most dreadful thing in the world at the time. But it is easy to be over-sensitive about errors. If you make too much fuss, then you stand a good chance of alienating the journalist. You have to decide how important it is to you or the company to get the error corrected in print. If it is a factual error which is, potentially at least, commercially damaging to your company then you should contact the journalist and explain the error. If it is sufficiently serious, you may get a correction. Another way, however, is to suggest that the journalist writes another story in which he includes the correct information, pointing out the mistake made in the previous story. This looks less damaging to a newspaper's credibility than a straightforward correction, while still ensuring that the correct information is included in print.

If a journalist refuses to correct a damaging factual error, then you should go above his head to the news or features editor. If still unsuccessful, then the editor is the last resort.

The problem arises in many cases, however, when the error is not a factual one but simply a matter of interpretation. The best recourse then, if you feel strongly enough, is to write a letter to the editor for publication. But do not use this as an opportunity to criticize the journalist. Instead, make it clear that your concern is a matter of interpretation. That way, you should still be able to maintain your relationship with the journalist concerned.

Radio and television

Radio and television are both highly effective means of getting your message across to target audiences. Yet at the same time there is no doubt that appearing on radio or television can strike fear into the soul of even the most successful corporate executive. What is it about television that can reduce grown men and women to seemingly helpless stuttering idiots?

The main cause is fear of the unknown. Dealing with the press – while it can be a novel experience – is almost certainly going to be carried out in an environment such as an office or restaurant which is at least familiar to you. Even telephone interviews with writing journalists make use of a means of communication with which you have had much practice. But television and radio is something completely different. It thrusts the normally composed business executive into an alien environment of microphones, blinding lights, clutter, hassle, and journalists who only seem to want to talk to you for two minutes at a time!

All the time, moreover, you are aware that you will be broadcasting to perhaps millions of complete strangers who may not be interested at all in what you have to say but who (if you are on television) may sit around with their family and friends ridiculing your tie or hairstyle! Small wonder, therefore, that appearing on radio and television is treated with suspicion by many senior business people.

What are the broadcast media all about – and how should you handle them?

Radio

In one sense, radio is an easier medium to learn to make use of since you only have to control your voice and not worry about how you look and act. But radio also has its own drawbacks for the novice interviewee. Radio is more immediate than television and there are a greater variety of opportunities to broadcast each day. Radio bulletins, for example, are going out on the hour, every hour, and there are several current affairs and news programmes each day which are possible to appear on.

The main broadcasting station on which business executives are likely to appear is BBC Radio Four, which is broadcast nationally. The early morning *Today* show is an especially important programme on which to appear, since it is listened to by a number of important decision-makers, including the Prime Minister! Radio Four also has a number of other current affairs programmes each day, as well as weekly feature programmes on which business people often appear (e.g. *Money Box*).

Apart from the main BBC national stations, there are many BBC and independent radio stations throughout the country. Research has shown that about six out of every ten local radio stations have some sort of weekly business programme. And do not forget the BBC's World Service programmes which can be a useful means of gaining publicity for your company or product in overseas markets. The Export Liaison Unit of the BBC's overseas radio services is there to help business people achieve just this sort of overseas publicity in the interests of promoting exports.

A popular type of programme (because it is relatively cheap to produce) is the phone-in which provides business people with considerable opportunity to get their case across as well as develop expertise in radio techniques. Bear in mind, however, that while the bulk of the listeners to such programmes will not have your expertise in the subject of the phone-in, some of the callers will. They will want to make a point on air – and often at your expense.

The key to broadcast programmes is to be prepared. Ask yourself what type of questions are likely to come up and formulate some basic answers. But keep them simple. You have to make your points simply and concisely, otherwise your listeners will switch off – either literally, or they will attend to something else. Avoid using jargon – you know what cash flow means, for example, but it is not a term which many listeners will be comfortable with.

When approached by a radio journalist for an interview – which may be recorded or broadcast live over your telephone or from a studio – find out as much as you can about the programme beforehand and the type of questions that may be asked. Concentrate on talking to just one person – not the millions who may be listening – and speak in a relaxed conversational manner, assuming the person is intelligent but not a specialist in your area.

Television

While you are statistically more likely to appear on a radio programme than on television, it is important not to fail to grasp the opportunities that are available on such programmes as BBC 2's popular *Money Programme* or the *Business* programme on Channel Four.

Television does funny things to people without them being able to do much about it. It makes people look much heavier than they really are, for example, so if you are a typical overweight executive it can add pounds to you on the screen. Your first contact with a television programme will often be a programme research assistant who will 'size' you up for television purposes and find out whether you have anything to say. Don't fall into the trap of trying to explain your point of view in detail – just come up with a few good key points. The researcher will be looking for how well you can put a simple idea across. Before agreeing to appear on a programme or be interviewed, find out who else will be there and what general type of questions are likely to be asked.

When you arrive at the television studio, don't expect to be fussed over. Everyone there has a job to do in order to get the programme out, and will not have time to worry about you. However, you will normally be put under the care of the same researcher or production assistant whom you have already met and who will make sure you visit the make-up department – to stop your nose shining on screen – and to take you into the studio.

Whatever type of programme it may be – a discussion programme with people of differing views or a straightforward interview – be aware that a camera will be focused on you all the time. Don't scratch your head or blow your nose, but sit calm and relaxed in your chair at all times.

Listen to the interview questions and come up with a succinct answer – you will probably only have 30 seconds or so in which to reply before the interviewer will cut in again with another question. Don't try to be funny – after all, professional comedians have trouble doing that – and be positive in your answers. Research has shown that while viewers may not remember what you say, they are impressed by the tone in which you say it!

Summary

Communication with the media is potentially one of the most effective forms of corporate communication, yet it is given a low priority by many business executives. The first part of this chapter outlines how journalists work, their priorities, and what they are looking for. It defines news and describes how journalists seek it, and how the media in general works, with a detailed illustration focused on the *Financial Times*.

The specific nature of the broadcast media is explained and the types of programmes which offer interviews to business executives are identified. Local, regional and national broadcasting are considered, not forgetting the powerful influence of the BBC's World Service in relation to overseas markets. The difficulties of speaking on radio and television programmes are considered with helpful tips on how to cope.

Successful media relationships depend on an understanding of how the media works and the role played by journalists. Although specific techniques can help in dealing with the media, the crucial factor is a desire to want to communicate your company's aims and objectives to your target groups through the channels of communication established by the media.

CHAPTER 6

COMMUNICATING THE COMPANY'S
RECORD OF ACHIEVEMENT

ᘿᗌ

W HEN your company is a success – in whatever sphere of activity – why not tell people about it? Surprisingly, many companies seem rather reluctant to communicate success to the important target groups. This reluctance may be due in some cases to a corporate sense of modesty, or a desire to keep a corporate low profile on the basis that 'putting our heads above the parapet will only attract more trouble than it's worth.' Both reasons are understandable – but hardly realistic in the modern-day world of change and communications. A more likely reason in many cases is simply that companies cannot be bothered.

Why talk about success?

There are a number of advantages to letting target groups know of your success:

1. Keeping shareholders and investors informed of your success is part of a pre-emptive approach to guard against an unwelcome takeover.
2. It is good for employee morale for staff to be told about success.
3. A successful company is often able to attract the best managers and staff simply because people generally like being associated with success.
4. Customers also like dealing with successful companies, especially in the retail and service sector.

What sort of successes should you talk about?

Obviously, your financial performance is an important success to communicate to the relevant target groups. Higher profits, sales, dividends and so on are all important yardsticks that tell people you are doing well.

A good example of communicating success relates to the unit trust industry. The Unit Trust Association decided to communicate the successful investment record of the industry in plain and simple terms to existing and potential investors. A working party was formed to study the way performance on unit trusts was assessed and described. This led to the development of a series of different categories for the funds, and measures to indicate movement of funds within the categories. Ensuring the use of these categories and measurements and their promotion at quarterly press briefings led in turn to the greater understanding of the nature of unit trusts and their benefits by the ordinary investor, who can now see that trusts, in the main, offer savings and investment advantages over some alternative investment products.

The Association also produced a number of other information tools, such as booklets and videos and a leaflet on how to enquire and complain about unit trusts. These have been made widely available to the general public and are very popular. In addition, the Association now has a Consumer Affairs Advisory Panel of distinguished consumer affairs specialists, which advises the Association on issues affecting the consumer. Professor Jim Gower in his report on financial services, which led to the introduction of the new Financial Services Act, paid tribute to the work of this Panel.

The way in which communicating success leads to further success is described in Case Study 1 on Grundfos Pumps Ltd on page 53. Their initiative to create a Better Business Club was an imaginative one.

Perhaps the most sensitive stories relating to communicating success are involved in the takeover situation. On page 56 the case history of the Waterford acquisition of Wedgwood is outlined in Case Study 2.

But, there are other sorts of successes too. When you have secured a notable contact or a new order, for example, it is worth spreading the good news. Similarly, if your company has helped with a community achievement then it is something of which you should be proud. Another important success which is often overlooked is when an executive in your company is appointed to a trade body or even a government 'quango', or is invited to speak at a prestigious conference.

Success is all around you – if you are only prepared to look for it.

How to go about communicating success

Increasingly, companies are beginning to recognize that the annual report and accounts – which used to be very boring documents indeed – are an important means of telling the financial community how well you are doing. The annual report is an ideal way of presenting the financial achievements of your company in an easily understandable form – using graphics and other forms of illustration to make profits or earnings per share growth more readily understandable to the lay reader.

Annual reports are also very useful for informing the share-holders and others exactly how well your products are performing in the marketplace. In addition, they can be used to show a new product range or explain a new service. The Burton Group, for example, has used its annual report to show its new range of fashions.

Increased awareness of annual reports in the communications function has, not surprisingly, led to a number of specialist designers offering their services in the production of these reports. The crucial point to remember is that the designers should not be allowed to let their imaginations run away with the project and the report should reflect your company's existing corporate identity.

As with the annual report, a special report to your employees can also be an important means of telling staff how well you are doing. Some companies are reluctant to provide such reports because they fear that such information will only encourage higher wage demands. As a company, however, you have to decide whether the people who have contributed to your success should not only be told about it but also be rewarded for it.

Many companies are finding it useful to produce a special report to customers. This should not only give details of your financial record but should show how the money is spent – customers do not want to get the impression that you are making money at their expense. Such a customer report can also be used to inform about improvements in the product or service you are offering.

Clearly, communicating success can also be achieved through normal advertising channels or through part of your public relations programme. It is often argued that the media does not want to know about successful companies – yet the experience of many in both the broadcast and written media is that success stories are simply not presented in an effective way.

Summary

Many companies are surprisingly reluctant to communicate success to their important target groups in terms of overall communication and some reasons for this reluctance have been considered in this chapter. The advantages of letting target groups know about your successes are identified and discussed. Consideration is then given to the ways in which success can be communicated, and why.

Don't hide your company's light under a bushel. Communicating success is essential to company planning to ensure that future success follows current success.

Case Study 1
COMMUNICATING SERVICE AND BACK-UP

Grundfos Pumps Ltd

Consultancy
Welbeck Public Relations Ltd

Dates
1984 ongoing

Summary
Water pumps for domestic central heating systems are the main product of Grundfos. These pumps are sold through a network of distributors and merchants, and bought by heating engineers and plumbers who install them. After the energy crises in the late 1970s, demand for efficient heating systems increased, as did Grundfos' share of the market. However, many cheap imported pumps were also available and installers tended to buy on the basis of price rather than quality. There was no direct link, other than through trade press advertising, between Grundfos and the installers, and some means of explaining the benefit of the Grundfos product was needed. This would show the advantage of dealing with a supportive manufacturer who understood the needs of the heating installer and who had all the engineering and back-up needed to produce a reliable product. Since the marketing arrangements would not be changed, the aim would be to encourage specification by the Grundfos name, and this led to the formation of the Grundfos Better Business Club.

Opportunity
Grundfos had a reputation for quality products and meeting its customers needs. It had determined a corporate policy of becoming market leader and was ready to adopt the stance of a leader and the responsibility which this involves. It would also provide the financial resources to implement any activity which would set it apart from and above its competitors.

Strategy
A research programme was carried out to discover more about the installers who purchased heating pumps from merchants. This showed that the majority were very small businesses – often one or two people who had grasped the entrepreneurial challenge. They operated locally, close to their homes, which was also their business address. Most were experienced plumbers but were not aware of some detailed technical matters related to heating systems and components and the majority were inexperienced managers. The Welbeck proposal was to introduce a Better Business Club which would provide them with some of the knowledge they lacked and would create an affinity with Grundfos. This would show Grundfos to be a caring and concerned company which was interested in the long-term development of installers' businesses. The provision of technical information on pumps was a conventional approach, but it was entirely original for a manufacturer to provide more generalized business information. Welbeck recognized that this information would be available from a variety of sources – banks, accountants, solicitors and government departments – but to concentrate on what would be useful for installers meant a great deal of sifting.

Programme
The first task would be to enrol members to the Better Business Club. No organised list was available, but a very rough estimate, based on classified listing in telephone and other directories, indicated at least 15,000 members. Reaching these could present major difficulties, but the support of merchants was enlisted. Point-of-sale displays and promotional material on pump packaging were used. The offer was free membership to a club which would provide a mailing pack every six months and a

direct line of communication for advice on pumps to Grundfos. The mailing consisted of a technical file sheet of systems and equipment and a circulation sheet covering business matters. Material for these was commissioned from specialist writers who dealt with VAT, income tax, employment law, publicity ideas, sources of capital and so forth. Additionally, a membership binder for the file sheets and an eight-page, full colour newspaper, *Pump Talk*, were included. This is a lively, bright publication containing application stories, news of new products, company information and occasional competitions.

In less than a year, some 12,000 installers had been registered as members of the club. These names are pruned occasionally to ensure that competitors are eliminated and only *bona fide* installers included. However, the primary purpose was to increase the market share and to obtain a close link between Grundfos and the installer, whilst the commercial link was through merchants. The results of the club can be judged from the fact that Grundfos now has over 65 per cent of the UK market for domestic circulator pumps, and this is despite a continuing increase of imported pumps and discounting by competitors. The need to create a response has been achieved by making special offers of equipment – computers and office machinery, and by asking members for their comments in a questionnaire form. This produced two positive views: firstly, that the club was useful and the information made a positive contribution to business growth and, secondly, that some practical seminars would be useful. Grundfos acted quickly in response and arranged a series of installer workshops for Better Business Club members. These were at venues around the country and included a morning meeting of ideas and advice on publicity, promotion and other ways of attracting customers. In the afternoon, Grundfos explained how systems could be improved and new products offered to customers. There were plenty of opportunities for discussion, questions and free-ranging exchanges of views. This series of seminars was of great value since it enabled both Grundfos and Welbeck to hear, first-hand, exactly what was happening in the tough end of the marketplace and what sort of support installers needed.

The Better Business Club is still being developed as it must be kept relevant in order to meet the immediate needs of installers. Feedback shows that it is welcomed and this can only be because it is geared around a practical understanding of problems 'at the coal face'. It has enabled Grundfos to create a strong identity with those who actually use its products, even though distribution is through third parties. However, in order to retain this interest, new and equally relevant elements must be added continually. This is an on-going process which Welbeck is leading for Grundfos and which positions them clearly as the market leader.

Case Study 2
THE WATERFORD ACQUISITION OF WEDGWOOD

Waterford

Consultancy
Charles Barker Traverse-Healy and Tim Dennehy and Associates

Dates of operation
October 1986 to December 1986

Summary
The essential role of communications in the Waterford Glass Group acquisition of Wedgwood was to develop a high profile for Waterford over a short period of time. The two consultancies were called in on 6 October 1986 and the offer was announced on 8 October.

After the frenetic activity of the first few days, the normal 60-day bid period was punctuated with high notes: the announcement of a 50 per cent stake on 9 October, the posting of the offer document to shareholders on 5 November, approval by Waterford shareholders on 28 November, and gaining of 85 per cent acceptances on 1 December when the offer became unconditional.

Opportunity
A profit leap by Wedgwood and a hostile bid by London International Group (LIG), which had been referred to the

Monopolies and Mergers Commission (MMC), meant that the timing of launching a bid for Wedgwood was unfortuitous.

Undaunted, Waterford embarked on this course for three very good reasons. First, LIG was said to be losing interest and looking for a buyer for its 10 per cent stake. Second, it was generally acknowledged that Wedgwood could not remain independent. Added to this was the third reason: Waterford, after a successful restructuring programme, accompanied by a proactive investor relations effort, was strong enough to contemplate an acquisition. It was a key 'plank' of the Waterford corporate strategy and the advancement by two years of the debt reduction plan made the acquisition possible financially. Most importantly, the marriage of Wedgwood and Waterford made strong commercial sense.

Problem

Wedgwood had shown itself to be fiercely independent. Indeed, it put up an effective rebuttal to the LIG bid, including parliamentary lobbying among the Staffordshire potteries' MPs.

Against Waterford also was its Irish origin. Finally, Waterford was determined that the acquisition should be by agreement. Before 8 October, and amid rising media speculation, there was little to suggest that Waterford would be greeted with open arms.

Strategy

The strategy, finalised over sandwiches at midnight on 6 October at Waterford's merchant bankers, S. G. Warburg & Co, dovetailed closely with the corporate objectives.

To combat perceived Wedgwood doubts, Warburgs and Waterford proposed a management structure which provided a high degree of autonomy for Wedgwood, and set up a British holding company to ensure continuing tax benefits for UK shareholders, while allowing Waterford access to the London capital markets.

The 'key' to the Wedgwood lock was the institutional investor audience. Yet, equally important, were Wedgwood management and employees, retail analysts and the financial media, in view of their opinion-forming role in an acquisition.

The thrust of the communications strategy was to raise awareness of the positive benefits of the acquisition: firstly, the advantages of a British holding company. Secondly, the advantages of a decentralized management structure and, thirdly, the commercial benefits and synergy created by the combined group.

Programme
As Warburgs and Waterford negotiated with Wedgwood and its merchant bank, Morgan Grenfell, on 6 and 7 October, mounting media speculation was met with informal press briefings by Charles Barker. Having convinced Waterford that a 'no comment' approach was unproductive, the statements, while informative, were guarded.

Agreement on the terms of a recommended offer by Waterford for Wedgwood was reached at 1.15 a.m. on 8 October. After a few hours of snatched sleep, a press conference was mounted at 30 Farringdon Street, London EC4 at 11.00 a.m. that same morning. Before a rapidly assembled room of journalists, armed with a Warburg press release and Waterford statement prepared by Charles Barker, Waterford announced that its £252.6 million offer was being unanimously recommended to shareholders by Wedgwood directors. Already acceptances by Wedgwood directors and other shareholders for 17.37 million shares had come in, giving Waterford a 38.2 per cent stake. Both parties then went on to explain the mutual benefits.

The offer provided the combination of two prestigious names in the world 'tabletop' industry; economies of scale in distribution, retailing, technology and production resources and marketing; benefits for Wedgwood in areas where Waterford was strongest and vice versa. The offer price also played its part. At £252.6 million, compared with LIG's £149 million, it was described by Paddy Hayes, Waterford's chairman, as the 'top end of fair'.

The Waterford board then flew across the Irish Sea to announce the offer at a press conference in Dublin. It was organized by Tim Dennehy and Associates, Waterford's long-standing PR consultancy in Ireland.

At the same time, all retail analysts and institutional investors in both companies were informed by an announcement circular. The Waterford share price shot up as a result.

The following day, positive and supportive news articles and features appeared in the national quality daily newspapers. The Lex column in the *Financial Times* on 9 October commented: 'Wedgwood decided to look after itself by finding an acceptable partner: Waterford Glass is not only a good fit, in the commercial sense, but has come up with terms at which most other bidders would have blanched.'

While the offer had the benefit of the backing of the Wedgwood board, Waterford's public profile still needed the quantum leap to make it credible and attractive to Wedgwood shareholders who were concerned about the future of their investments.

Features and interviews were organized for Waterford chairman, Paddy Hayes, and finance director, Anthony Brophy, with the *Financial Times* management page, the 'Mammon' profile in the *Observer*, Channel Four '*Business Programme*', *Financial Weekly* and the American business magazine, *Forbes*, enabling Waterford to reach its US ADR shareholders.

In a company profile by Jonathan Gregson, *Financial Weekly* commented: 'From a marketing point of view this seems to be a marriage made in heaven. The merged group will be a world leader in luxury tableware sales. Already great things are expected of the union.' Paddy Hayes and Anthony Brophy also met the main institutional shareholders, fund managers and brokers, in order to explain the advantages of the offer.

On 9 October, Waterford announced that it spoke for more than 50 per cent of the issued share capital of Wedgwood. The press release was sent to analysts and institutional investors as well as to city editors and business finance magazines.

The next two weeks saw the completion of the offer document, produced by Charles Barker City. On 5 November, it was sent to both Wedgwood and Waterford shareholders. Waterford convened an extraordinary meeting, on 28 November in Dublin, at which shareholders approved the terms of the offer.

On 1 December, Charles Barker issued a press release which read: 'Waterford announces that, at 3 p.m. on 28 November 1986, the acceptances of the offer for Wedgwood had been received in respect of 39,822,139 Wedgwood shares, representing 87.5 per cent.' The offer had now become unconditional.

Conclusion

The root to the successful Waterford acquisition lay in a sound corporate strategy. It overcame the concerns of Wedgwood with original solutions. The accompanying press and investor relations programmes heightened awareness of the benefits at a critical time for Waterford when, without such support, they might have gone by default.

Wedgwood employees had, during the time of the bid, the comfort of their board's recommendation. After the take-over, a conference of Wedgwood managers was called by Waterford. It requested the active contribution of managers to the Wedgwood corporate strategy, along the lines of the Waterford ethos: what Paddy Hayes calls 'participative management'.

The result, according to an Irish investment banker quoted in *Forbes*, is that: 'Waterford is leaving Dublin behind. They're playing the big game now.' The *Financial Times* also noted: 'When an Irish company has established a widely acclaimed name and reputation it seems to have little option but to disregard its home economy as a major route to expansion and instead turn to world markets.'

CHAPTER 7

KEY RELATIONSHIPS

ℰ∼℺

T HE essence of successful communications is reaching those people that you want to hear your message. They may not heed the message but at least they will have been given the opportunity to hear what you have to say. Given this, it is surprising that so many communications are wasted, mainly because the wrong target is being addressed.

Targeting is the name of the game in the communications business. Identifying the group you want to reach depends on knowing exactly what the message is that you want to put across. If you want to influence MPs about legislation that may affect your company or industry, then it is clearly pointless to place advertisements or promote editorial in mass-circulation consumer magazines. Similarly, sales of cosmetics are obviously not going to be enhanced by a write-up or advertisement in the *Investors Chronicle*.

What are the key target groups?

Customers

Consumers are the bedrock of most communication campaigns. Without someone to buy your products, your company will eventually go out of business. But what sort of consumers do you want to reach? What is their age, sex, interests, and socio-economic group?

It is important to identify closely the sub-sectors of the consumer market you are trying to reach in order to clarify your communications strategy. If your target group, for example, is 24–45 year old males, then securing mentions on mid-morning local radio chat shows would not reach them very effectively.

Customers can be approached in a number of ways. Don't forget, for example, that they are already aware of your company and product through actually being customers. Thus you can reach them every time they are involved with you, through a message on the product or sales receipt, for instance, but bear in mind that you need the goodwill of your customers, so it is important not to bombard them with useless information!

Reaching customers can also be achieved in a varity of non-editorial ways. Live events, from fashion shows to cookery demonstrations, are a useful technique – as are exhibitions at consumer shows or giving talks to consumer interest groups. A simple demonstration evening, for example, for a new food product at which consumers receive vouchers redeemable at local stockists not only builds goodwill but also encourages product trial.

An example of how to communicate well with customers and potential customers in a specific age group is illustrated in Case Study 1 on page 67. Brand managers of Cinzano wanted to create specific awareness in their target market of 18–25 year olds. Through the creation of a national consumer event they did just that. Planning and targeting, however, had to be quite specific to get the desired result.

Employees

Although it seems obvious that your own staff is one of the primary groups to communicate with, many companies still only pay lip service to the concept of employee communications. The benefit of good communications with employees is obvious – improved morale and productivity. Yet many companies only consider telling staff what is happening when a crisis develops – when redundancies have to be announced, for example, or a takeover bid for the company has been made. Communicating with employees during times of crisis when no previous communication channels have been opened is hardly guaranteed to be successful.

While various sophisticated systems for employee communications exist – such as briefing teams of employees – the successful systems are those in which management tell the truth to their employees and are committed to keeping them informed. In many cases, a simple newsletter produced regularly is probably one of the most effective techniques available. It does not have to be expensively produced – it normally can be typed and printed within a normal office – but it does have to be honest.

A good move is to appoint an editorial board from employees to help ensure that the newsletter maintains its editorial integrity. If possible, appoint to such a board those employees who are natural sources of the office grapevine. If they know what you want to say in a newsletter first, then there is a good chance that they will relay this information on through the grapevine as well as the newsletter.

Communicating with employees can be all the more sensitive when the company is planning a major strategic change in its operation which will affect large numbers of employees. Case Study 2 on page 69 outlines how Courage planned the change of operation of its tied house estate at the beginning of 1987, transferring 900 of its 1300 managed pubs to tenancy. The problem was at three levels. The company needed acceptance from at least 60 per cent of those affected to avoid disruption to the operation of its tied estate. It also needed to recognize the likely attitude of the National Association of Licensed House Managers (NALHM), which stood to lose a significant proportion of its membership. In addition Courage needed to ensure continued commitment from those running the pubs that would remain managed. A central theme, 'Enterprise 87', was adopted to reflect the spirit of progress the change heralded. Face-to-face briefings recognized the need for people to be personally informed and back-up materials were produced, with two separate but complementary communications packages, geared to the needs of the separate audiences and highlighting the opportunities to each. The strategy also included recognition of the importance of timing and confidentiality at all stages of the operation. The results achieved were impressive and 92 per cent of managers accepted the transfer tenancy within seven days of the announcement, despite opposition and lobbying. The remaining managers also responded positively.

A further illustration of raising a company's profile with its existing and potential customers and also with its employees is given in Case Study 3 on page 71. Geest, Britain's ninth largest private company, with a turnover of £350 million, decided to use the occasion of their 50th anniversary to raise profile – with an eye to future flotation. The strategy focused on the golden jubilee and included development of the corporate image and the relaunch of the company's internal publication in order to extend employees' awareness of the corporate view and the key issues affecting the business. The results achieved were again impressive and the Geest flotation was one of the most successful of 1986, while a high proportion of its staff – over 30 per cent – took up share options in the company.

Investors

It was not so long ago that companies considered their shareholders as one of the last groups of people they should keep informed. The management view was that as long as the dividend and share price was right, there was little point in keeping investors informed. But all that changed in the 1980s as a result of predatory takeover attempts. Companies now increasingly keep not only their existing shareholders well informed of development, but also potential shareholders such as city analysts and institutions.

The financial community can be approached in a number of ways: through editorial comment in financial newspapers and magazines; through the annual report and accounts; or through direct mailing of existing or potential shareholders.

Editorial comment is one of the most effective means of communications with investors since as well as providing information it also gives independent comment. It is crucial, therefore, that you ensure that you reach those financial journalists who write such comments and make sure that they are kept well informed of your activities.

Communication can also be used most effectively to increase awareness of the true potential of an organization, particularly amongst investors – both existing and future. Case Study 4 on page 73 concerns the Brent Walker Group and shows how a programme was planned to combat low levels of spontaneous awareness of Brent Walker among leading fund managers and city analysts, to increase understanding of the Group and to position the company as a well-managed, stable and profitable organization. Both advertising and public relations techniques were used and the company's corporate identity was also refurbished. Results reflected the success of the operation and within six months the share price had risen by over 45 per cent.

Another successful programme of communication with shareholders is considered in Case Study 5 on page 76. This features Barker & Dobson and a programme which was planned and implemented in 1985. Objectives were to counter poor City perception, poor performance – shareholders had watched the value of their holdings fall by 90 per cent in the previous 10 years – and a record of poor management. In this case the communication programme focused on the appointment of a new Chairman and Chief Executive who came to the job with an impressive track record of success.

Central government

Influencing ministers, MPs, and civil servants can be vital for the success or failure of your company or industry. Although the United Kingdom is not yet at the same lobbying stage as the United States, influencing these key decision-makers requires subtlety.

Every company at some stage will be affected by central government decisions – ranging from planning enquiries through to changes in the rates and taxes system. Methods used to change the official mind are numerous, but mainly centre on personal contacts and achieving favourable editorial in the quality press that will be read by politicians and civil servants.

It is not necessary to be a sophisticated lobbyist to take advantage of contacts. Your local MP, for example, will be very interested in issues which affect employment in his constituency, so do not hesitate to tell him about local or national government projects which you think could make your company less profitable or have to shed jobs. Your trade association, moreover, may have its own links with MPs and civil servants which can be used to further your cause, even if the trade association itself does not want to take up the issue.

Local government

Just as central government can be influenced, so local authorities play an equally important role in the commercial world. Major super-markets, for example, have for some years realized that it is crucial to spell out to local authorities the benefits of a new superstore development on local employment. Ensuring that local authorities are aware of your point of view is not in any way underhand: you feel your case is justified, so why not put it effectively?

Councillors representing your business district should be approached with any problem or issue that you may have. Beware, however, of offering excessive hospitality since this could be misconstrued if any allegations of bribery or corruption should arise at a later date.

If your company is a major employer or significant business in part of a city or town, then consider improving local goodwill through such means as sponsorship or improvements to local amenities. A local community on your side can often help with staff recruitment and to influence local authorities.

A good example of how a company can plan a communications programme which helps the community within which it is operating,

is that of the TSB Trust Company's operation in Andover. This is
featured in Case Study 6 on page 79. It describes how a multi-purpose
and multi-level campaign to include sponsorship of the local railway
station can positively contribute to the local community.

Business-to-business

Other companies are sometimes forgotten as a target group in their
own right. When taking trade space at an exhibition, for example,
don't rely on your potential business customers just finding you by
chance – tell them in advance when and where you will be.

Within your distribution chain from factory to consumer there
are a number of key groups to consider. Retailers, wholesalers,
transport operations – all are targets you want to reach, not only to
engender confidence in your products but also to offer promotional
support.

The media

Press, radio, and television are, of course, crucial targets to reach. Yet
the media is split into many component parts – national and local
newspapers, radio and television stations, for example. In identifying
target groups within the media, therefore, it is especially important
to find the section that most clearly fits in with the audiences you
are trying to reach. (See Chapter 5 for a discussion of ways of
communicating with the media in more detail. The case studies
at the end of this chapter also provide an insight into using the
media.)

Summary

The key to successful communications is to target the appropriate
group or groups, which could be customers, employees, investors,
central and local government, business-to-business and the media.
Each of the possible target groups has been discussed in detail and
suggestions made as to how they should be approached. The trend
towards narrow targeting will probably be the most used communications technique of the 1990s. The following case histories illustrate
the points made above:

Case Study 1
COMMUNICATING WITH CUSTOMERS

International Distillers and Vintners (Cinzano)

Consultancy
Welbeck Public Relations Ltd.

Dates
September 1986 to March 1987.

Summary
Brand managers wanted an original campaign aimed at the particular interests of the target market: 18–25 year old men and women. This would create added sales to complement the existing core market of women aged over 35. A national consumer event was devised which would have specific appeal and provide an opportunity for both regional and national editorial publicity. Additionally, it would encourage sales outlets to test demand and then stock this vermouth brand. The project, a Model of the Year competition, was run in discos throughout the United Kingdom. This attracted the desired audience in considerable numbers as well as extensive publicity. The emphasis was on quality, so attention to detail was especially important. The first prize was a one-year modelling contract in the United States and this underlined the sponsor's seriousness.

Opportunity
Welbeck created a national consumer event not only to generate extensive publicity for the brand name, but also to provide sampling opportunities for the target group in surroundings familiar to them. The model competition would satisfy individual aspirations under the aegis of the brand. Additionally, although only girls would be eligible for prizes, their partners would be able to share in the social aspects of the events.

Programme
The competition was launched in conjunction with *Today* newspaper using colour editorial pages. Additionally appropriate

trade and consumer publications were mailed with releases. Relevant local newspapers where regional heats would take place were contacted and interest generated. Thirteen disco clubs throughout the country were selected for these heats and entries co-ordinated. Administration – all of which was handled by Welbeck – included arrangements for the actual staging, rehearsals and media coverage. For some locations, this was the first time such an event had been staged, so all facilities had to be provided ranging from catwalks to lighting. The judging was done by a team of fashion, beauty and home interest specialists, supported by a representative of Cinzano. The organization of groups to provide this service throughout the country, judging guidelines and back-up material was all provided by Welbeck. A standard procedure for publicity at each of the 13 venues was devised, to cover both pre- and post-event media requirements. This included not only press local to the actual disco club, but also to the competing girls who must have travelled some distance to take part. Welbeck concentrated on developing close direct contact with the local press and followed up all releases with telephone calls. The value of this was borne out in the media coverage both before and after each event. This was especially important to ensure a good attendance of the target age groups at the heats where sampling would be available. Media included radio and television as well as newspapers with many pre-event broadcasts and interviews after the heats in support of news bulletin items announcing results.

Throughout the period of the regional heats, interest in the finals was developed to make it an important occasion for the winners. The prizes were carefully chosen; for example, they would receive a car as well as the modelling contract in the United States. The runner-up would have jewellery and the third prize was a Caribbean holiday for two.

The choice of venue for the final was given as much careful attention as the rest of the competition. The aim was to find somewhere different from the usual locations and, if possible, redolent of the showbiz theme. After much research, the Limehouse Studios in London's Docklands was chosen. This would enable the organizers to stage a suitably dramatic final, to entertain media and trade guests and also to give the finalists an impression of the atmosphere created at a big fashion event. Welbeck's role at the final was total – organizing costumes, rehearsals, entertainment, catering, transport and security. The lead-up included a press call for the fashion and drinks trade press, radio and television interviews and photography on the eve of the finals. Links were established with broadcast media local to the finalists and maintained so that news of their girls would be known immediately the results were announced. This pre-planning meant that the winner, who came from Yorkshire, was featured on both the BBC and independent television magazine programmes in that area. It also ensured that the presentation of the competition and the role of the sponsor – with subsequent brand mention – would be thorough. Newspapers received results with photographs overnight via a round-the-clock press office operated by Welbeck. Maintaining the pressure, the winner took part, the following day, in interviews previously arranged with the *Daily Express*, the *Sun*, the *People* and *Today*. These newspapers were particularly selected since their reader profile included a major proportion of the target 18-35 male/female group.

Case Study 2
COMMUNICATING WITH EMPLOYEES

Courage Ltd

Consultancy
Paragon Communications plc

Dates
November 1986 to January 1987

Summary
Courage Ltd undertook a major strategic change in the operation of its tied house estate at the beginning of 1987, transferring 900 of its 1300 managed pubs to tenancy. The pub managers affected were to be offered a six-month transfer tenancy on special terms, leading (with the agreement of both sides) to the offer of a full

tenancy on normal terms. The remaining pubs were to stay under
existing management, becoming the flagships of the organization and spearheading new retailing developments.

Paragon was appointed less than eight weeks before the
announcement was due to be made and in that time devised and
produced a complete internal communications programme. It
was aimed at securing the commitment of senior managers to the
plans and preparing them for 'down the line' briefing responsibilities; gaining agreement to the transfer tenancy from those
affected and maintaining support and motivation from those
who would remain as managers.

Problem
Courage *needed* acceptance for the transfer tenancy from at least
60 per cent of those affected to avoid disruption to the operation
of its tied estate. There would inevitably be opposition, not least
from the National Association of Licensed House Managers
(NALHM), which stood to lose a significant proportion of its
membership. Those running the pubs that would remain
managed were also a key target audience as their continued
commitment and motivation were commercially essential.

Strategy
Paragon made the following recommendations:

1. The adoption of the theme 'Enterprise 87' to reflect the spirit
   of progress the changes heralded – both for the company and
   individuals.
2. Emphasis on face-to-face 'personalized' briefing for all those
   affected.
3. Provision of materials to ensure these briefings were consistent throughout the organization.
4. Two separate, but complementary communications packages,
   geared to the needs of both audiences – transfer tenants and
   managers – highlighting to each the opportunities available.
5. Absolute confidentiality until the formal announcement.

Programme
The material produced included the structure and visual support
for briefing of senior management together with a 'how to do it'

section covering their onward communications responsibilities and procedures. Transfer tenants and remaining managers were to be briefed at 70 simultaneous meetings throughout the country. There were two versions of the material supplied for these meetings – one for transfer tenants and one for remaining managers – which included videos, overhead presentation kits, and personalized information packs containing brochures and other relevant information. For transfer tenants it included individual information such as their pub rent and stock valuation and a *Running Your Own Business* leaflet.

Results
The success of the communications programme was apparent just seven days after the announcement when 92 per cent of managers had accepted the transfer tenancy – despite vigorous opposition and lobbying from their union – and the remaining managers responded enthusiastically to the move. Courage trade projects director who was responsible for the implementation of the change said:

> 'Even some of the critics were impressed by the organization and communication that helped make the project progress so smoothly. We were delighted with the speed and professionalism with which Paragon reacted to our needs and the results achieved certainly justify their slogan that 'excellence reaps its just rewards'.

Case Study 3
COMMUNICATING WITH CUSTOMERS AND EMPLOYEES

Geest

Consultancy
Paragon Communications plc

Dates
September 1985 to November 1986

Summary
On the eve of its fiftieth anniversary, Britain's ninth-largest

private company – with a turnover of £350 million – appointed Paragon and advertising agents Broadbents in order to raise its profile with existing and potential customers and improve communications with employees. With an eye to its future flotation, the company also asked Paragon to address the City among its key target groups.

Opportunity
Paragon commissioned research among the principal target groups which highlighted the fact that Geest was viewed largely as a one-product company (bananas) and that those with regular dealings with the organization had no real conception of its size and capabilities. The same was true of many of its 4,000 staff, particularly those whose companies had been taken over by Geest. Basically, the opportunity existed to inform the target groups that Geest was and continues to be a market leader in the field of fresh produce, a major supplier of houseplants, and a leading manufacturer of salad dishes and chilled foods for supermarket multiples.

Strategy
In collaboration with Broadbents, Paragon devised a corporate PR strategy as follows:

1. Build a public relations programme around the golden jubilee in order to focus trade and City awareness on the company's market leadership and achievements.
2. Develop the corporate image to reflect its modern approach and success with the high street multiples in particular.
3. Relaunch the company's internal publication in order to extend awareness of the corporate view and the key issues affecting the business.

Programme
As part of the strategy, the following activities were undertaken by Paragon during the course of the next nine months:

1. Helped to create a new corporate identity supported by a comprehensive press pack covering company profile, industry data, management profiles and a selection of photographs depicting key aspects of the business.

2. Organized media training sessions for senior directors who were selected as company spokesmen.
3. Arranged a series of face-to-face briefings on the company with leading trade and business publications. This included the creation of a company tour and hospitality policy at the headquarters in Spalding, Lincolnshire.
4. Developed a presentation format for briefing analysts and City journalists in order to build up interest before the announcement to go public.
5. Sustained interest in Geest through a series of high-profile anniversary events, including a gala dinner in London attended by government ministers and top customers.
6. Increased the frequency and professionalism of the company newspaper *Outlook*, which became a major communications vehicle during the period leading to flotation.
7. Paragon also advised Geest on its communications with customers and prepared reserve statements on contentious issues affecting the fresh produce industry.

Results
By the time Geest came to float on the London Stock Exchange in November 1986, the company was known as much more than just a banana importer among all the target groups identified at the start of the campaign. So much so, that the company's prospects for growth in the area of chilled foods and prepared recipe dishes were the major talking point of analysts' reports on the sale prospectus. The Geest flotation was one of the most successful of 1986 and a high proportion of its staff – over 30 per cent – took up their options on shares in the company.

Case Study 4
COMMUNICATING WITH INVESTORS

The Brent Walker Group

Consultancy
Valin Pollen

Date
Spring 1986

Problem
Founded in 1967, the original Brent Walker company quickly expanded from its base in fast-food catering into banqueting, country clubs, stadium management and projects such as the Brent Cross shopping centre, as well as film, television and video production. Despite this success, past relations with the City had not always been fortunate.

In 1983, Chairman George Walker and the board of directors bought out the public shareholding, returning the Group to private company status. Despite the potential of major new projects, such as the £200 million redevelopment of Brighton Marina, the market's response did not meet expectations when the Group refloated in June 1985, and by December 1985 the share price had fallen from 130p to 103p.

Objectives
An initial pilot study commissioned by Valin Pollen's research and planning unit clearly identified the need to increase awareness of the true potential of the group and the scope and success of its activities. Valin Pollen were formally appointed to develop an integrated programme of communications on behalf of the Brent Walker Group. This was timed to utilize the momentum of the Group's excellent recent financial performance and of leading developments such as Brighton Marina in order to achieve the following:

1. Combat low levels of spontaneous awareness of Brent Walker among leading fund managers and City analysts.
2. Increase understanding of the Group and its varied leisure-related business activities and thus encourage more positive attitudes towards it.
3. Position Brent Walker as a well-managed, stable and profitable company.

Action
Research showed that to achieve this ultimate objective the

communications programme had to fulfil a number of criteria as follows:

1. In the short term, information about the Group would immediately raise its profile, but a constant flow of detailed information would have to follow as new developments arose.
2. Due to the Group's complex divisional structure, any corporate message had to be simple, precise and relevant.
3. Deep-seated attitudes are the most difficult to change; thus the campaign had to be provocative, full of impact and persuasive.
4. The negative emotional attitudes towards the Group could be overcome with factually-based messages emphasizing tangible values.

To maximize impact, the communications mix centred on a major corporate advertising campaign in a two-paper schedule, comprising the *Financial Times* and *Sunday Times*. This was supported with an integrated programme of press and investor relations, targeted mailings, a programme of journalist and analyst lunches and tours of the Group's major operations.

Valin Pollen also undertook a refurbishment of the Group's corporate identity to reflect a personality more commensurate with the Group's target audiences and its recent initiatives into more sophisticated markets.

Result
Six months after Valin Pollen's appointment, Brent Walker's share price had risen by over 45 per cent, adding more than £12 million to the Group's market capitalization, and significantly out-performing the FT All-Share Index.

Such progress was achieved through the commercial efforts of the client and the proper communication by the agency of their successes, with the joint result that awareness of the Group as a whole and its potential as an investment vehicle has been effectively promoted.

Although further tracking of shifts in awareness and attitudes has yet to be completed, the improved share performance, together with extensive supportive press commentary, indicate that a major and positive change in attitudes has been achieved.

Case Study 5
COMMUNICATING WITH SHAREHOLDERS

Barker & Dobson

Consultancy
Biss Lancaster

Date
May 1985

Problem
City perception of the Barker & Dobson Group plc was poor.
The company had suffered losses in five years out of ten due to
involvement in a series of disastrous diversifications. Shareholders had watched the value of their holdings fall by 90 per cent
in the previous ten years. There was a past history of poor
management.

Opportunity
The installation of the retail-experienced Mr John Fletcher as
Chairman and Chief Executive with a track record of huge
success with Asda and Oriel.

Corporate profile
It was acknowledged the City perception of a company and its
strategy depended heavily on the front man and the management
team. John Fletcher, a man with an impressive track record with
several retail organizations, already had a good reputation within
the City. It was decided to target relevant media with an ongoing
corporate communication programme that would ultimately
increase investor awareness whilst at the same time reassure
existing shareholders of the dramatic turnaround that was to
come.

Programme
Initial moves were made to inform the media of John Fletcher's
acceptance of chairmanship of the Board. The news was
welcomed by a temporary increase in Barker & Dobson's share

price. The quality nationals were invited to meet John Fletcher personally via a detailed introduction letter, which resulted in a series of interviews including one in the *Financial Times*. Press releases were sent to the daily financial and trade press of appointments to the Board, reinforcing Fletcher's intention of establishing a strong, incisive Board that was to maintain a proper day-to-day management role.

Results
The accolade of City Personality Award to John Fletcher in August 1986, was a tribute to his achievements in building up a diversified group. Corporate profiles on John Fletcher appeared in key financial/corporate publications such as *Investors Chronicle*, *Director*, *Financial Decisions* and *Management Today* as well as *Marketing Week*, all outlining the complete Barker & Dobson story.

Financial activity
Between May 1985 and April 1986, the immediate financial problems facing John Fletcher were resolved. The sale of Lewis Meeson (July 1985) was approved by the shareholders and was to raise £10 million that would settle immediate indebtedness. The acquisition of James Keiller and Sons Ltd reassured shareholders and the City of Fletcher's intention of concentrating on Barker & Dobson's traditional business.

Programme
Press releases were sent out to the financial press announcing the Board's intentions, so that coverage coincided with shareholders' receipt of their legal documentation concerning the following:

1. Disposal of the Lewis Meeson Group.
2. Rights issue to raise £5.2 million for the acquisition of Keiller.
3. Rights issue to raise £69.9 million for the acquisition of Budgen.
4. Small shareholders offer.
5. Share consolidation one for 10.

A circular of background information was sent out to analysts and key national press to supplement the issued press releases,

outlining the changed structure of the Group. In recognition of
the new style Group, after the acquisition of Budgen, a frank,
open *Fact Book* was produced and sent to key analysts, outlining
the major moves made towards the diversification of the
formerly confectionery-orientated business to a food-related
trading company and also outlining future strategies.

Both 1985 and 1986 results were made known to shareholders
and investors through the annual reports and the media.

The coverage gained on the results of 1986 clearly demonstrated the move from the City's expectations of bad performance in 1985 to a mood of confidence inspired by the
rationalization of the confectionery division and successful
diversification towards food retailing.

Both 1985 and 1986 reports and accounts, the traditional tool
of communication, sought to instil shareholder confidence
through their directness of approach. The 1985 report and
accounts were low key and inexpensive. By contrast the 1986 set
of accounts were designed to be a major statement to investors,
and the 1986 annual report was intended to reflect the successful
turnaround of the Group to profitability, achieved by John
Fletcher and his management team.

The 1986 Annual General Meeting was held in London for the
first time and was intended to signal to the target audience of
investors and existing shareholders that the Barker & Dobson
Group plc was now a viable entity and a serious investment.

Corporate video
This was compiled with the client and produced by Falkman
Films in April 1987. It was felt that the growth and changed
nature of Barker & Dobson Group needed to be encapsulated in
visual form and circulated to interested institutions and could also
be used to further trade. Its first showing was at the AGM in May
1987 where it received a warm reception both from shareholders
and representatives of the institutional investors that attended.

Case Study 6
COMMUNICATING WITH STAFF AND WITH THE LOCAL COMMUNITY

TSB Trust Company in Andover

Dates
1973 to 1987.

Opportunity
TSB Trust Company came to Andover from London in 1973. At that time the company totalled approximately 40 people and was six years old as the unit trust and insurance offshoot of the TSB Group. Its main purpose was to provide TSB banking customers with access to additional personal financial services which, otherwise, they would be seeking outside the TSB Group.

By 1987 the TSB Trust Co. has become the largest employer in Andover with over 1500 staff plus another 500 sales representatives in the field. It built a new head office in 1978 and extended it in 1981. In 1983 the computer centre was opened. Such was the company's rate of growth that by 1985 a 15-acre site in Andover had been acquired and in the summer of 1987 a whole new corporate head office and residential training centre was opened, with a new computer centre on an adjacent site scheduled for 1988.

Such rapid growth in the context of staff employed – as opposed to success in business – provides the background to two particular topics. One is staff communication and the importance ascribed to it by the company; the other concerned relationships with the host community – Andover – the town, the people, the local media, local authority and local institutions.

Communication with staff
The company prides itself on the success of its efforts to ensure that staff communication is effective. It is not unnatural, of course, that 'effective communication' will still leave untouched the two extreme views that people are either insufficiently informed and, the diametrically opposite, over informed!

Throughout management there is an awareness that the

company has a culture and management works hard to ensure that staff generally recognize the key elements of the culture. A frequent spontaneous response is that the company, though successful and very hard working, is friendly. From this comes the feeling that the company and its staff are communicative and that authority is well delegated to various and appropriate levels of departmental staff. In other words, if the ball is given to someone he, or she, is expected to run with it! The company ethos, therefore, is that while the company is market driven and the objective is profit and success, hard work in comfortable surroundings and with good rewards, removes any sense of daily drudgery.

The company has several ways of communicating business and social information and messages. Every month in every department a system of briefing groups is implemented. Briefing group notes are agreed at director and senior executive level and these are used and extended if necessary, as the basis of information as the briefings cascade down the line and stimulate questions back up the line. Briefing group notes cover topics of interest and significance emanating from TSB Group head office as well as dealing with local operational matters.

Social news is covered by the monthly house newspaper *Chatterbox* now in its eleventh year. Although not exclusively so, the newspaper, run by a professional full-time journalist/editor, also covers business and policy matters but in a journalistic style. The print run of 2000 is invariably fully taken up. Head office locations are served by judiciously placed dispensers and all staff help themselves. Additional internal communication, on an ad hoc basis, is effected through a system of circulars. An active sports and social club also makes use of *Chatterbox*, in addition to making announcements by posters and newsletters.

The company also communicates with the rest of the TSB Group through a glossy quarterly A4 magazine, *Portfolio*, which is distributed by TSB bank branch managers and covers product, business, industry and personality news and information.

Finally, in the list of publications prepared for staff, comes the annual *Employee Report*, which appears nearly simultaneously with the company's annual report and accounts. This successful and popular publication is produced by a committee of staff members, usually volunteers, with the editor of the house newspaper providing only a consultancy service. This self-help publication is widely appreciated and the level of response to questionnaires included with the *Employee Report* proves the fact.

The annual report and accounts document itself is distributed to all management and to all other group companies and is always available for all staff members. Similarly, publications such as the company's *Corporate Brochure* are also distributed to management and to other group companies.

TSB Group itself has a group newspaper call *Banknotes*, which is distributed throughout all group locations.

Community relations

It is axiomatic that any organization that is the largest employer in a town acquires a high profile, particularly if it is one which bears a well-known national emblem such as the TSB. A natural consequence of a high profile is the frequency with which individuals and organizations approach the company for financial support for a wide variety of projects, charities, events and the like.

Whilst the company will always do its best to assist, the frequency of such requests creates the need for selection with differing criteria for the various categories identified. For example, purely charitable donations constitutes one category within which selection must be made. Town projects is another. Cultural events and youth groups are two more examples. Each category generates far more demand than the company can ever satisfy but each category does receive a share of what is available in the budget.

The company's desire to help where it can is seen as beneficial not only by the townspeople but also helps maintain good relations with the local authority which perceive it not only as a good employer and sound contributor to the town's economic and social fabric but also as responsive to needs which the local authority is not always able to help meet to the extent it would like.

Some examples of the company's larger involvements will provide an idea of how it supports the community in a meaningful way:

ANDOVER STATION

Like many railway stations the one at Andover was a dilapidated and unimpressive introduction to the town for anyone arriving by train. The building itself was sound and of some interest but surrounded by tacked on 'temporary' buildings which had acquired permanency. In 1985 the TSB Trust Co. became aware of the British Rail 'Partnership' scheme which involved participation with BR on a 50/50 basis in the renovation of stations. The scheme was generally aimed at companies with head offices in locations where the station was either adjacent to the company offices or, as in this case, a town amenity of both interest and usefulness as much to the company as to the community.

Following newspaper coverage of the Friary Meux renovation at Godalming, the company's head office, an interest was expressed in joining BR in improving Andover. BR offered very straightforward sponsorship benefits in terms of opportunities for associating the name with the renovation and also offered its standard terms under a 'Partnership' deal of using company colours, hence the current appearance of Andover station in a combination of blue, gold, white and black.

Of particular interest is the fact that having sold TSB Trust Co. the concept of renovating the platforms on the passenger side of the station, BR was able to interest the local authority in sharing the renovation and redesign of the frontage of the building, new carparks and forecourt. This was a successful joint operation which additionally involved the Manpower Services Commission, who assisted with the landscaping of those parts of the station which had previously been unused track beds.

ANDOVER MUSEUM OF THE IRON AGE

Andover has had a museum for many years but not one which was capable of showing off properly the results of the excavations of the Danebury Hill Fort, conducted over many years by Professor Barry Cunliffe of the Institute of Archeology in Oxford.

In 1985 a scheme was approved by Hampshire County Council, the Test Valley Borough Council (the local authority), and other interested bodies, to adapt the old school building adjoining Andover Museum and to create a new museum with an

'Iron Age' environment to house a display of artefacts from the Danebury diggings. The displays would be illuminated to modern museum design standards with supporting texts interestingly written without loss of intellectual soundness. County and Borough offered to meet their commitments to the scheme by respectively handing over the property and undertaking the conversions. The actual museum would depend on commercial sponsorship and it would require evidence of commitments on that score before County and Borough would confirm their positions.

To attract commercial sponsorship would require a properly designed and attractive appeal brochure. It was at this 'seedcorn' stage that TSB Trust Co. accepted a proposal to sponsor the brochure and become 'lead' sponsors for £10,000. The museum organizers were eventually able to meet the County and the Borough conditions regarding sponsorship evidence and the museum was completed. Lord Denning performed the opening ceremony. Since making the original donation of £10,000, TSB Trust Co. has contributed a further £7,000 towards the production, jointly with Hampshire County Council, of a high quality museum guide.

The existence of the Iron Age Museum in Andover adds to the tourist attractions as well as drawing in enthusiasts, amateur and professional archeologists, historians and related groups. All this is good for Andover and the area in terms of raising its profile as a visitor destination.

ANDOVER FESTIVAL

In September 1985 the first Andover Festival of Arts and Wine took place. The title has since been shortened to the Andover Festival and the organizers are gradually building up a reputation for running a festival that can attract artists and audience, avoid ending up with too great a loss, can attract commercial sponsorship and can be seen as bringing something to Andover which Salisbury and Newbury have been enjoying for years. It is a week-long festival, embodying visual and performing arts, ranging from low through middle to high brow to cater for the broad range of tastes in Andover, often regarded as a cultural desert due to the proximity of Salisbury, Newbury and Winchester.

TSB Trust Co. was approached at the very beginning and remains the largest sponsor in cash terms at a level of around £8,000. The company accepted the organizers' view that there was a place for a festival which could be a socially cohesive force in what is a socially diverse community. Anything which could enhance the quality of life in Andover and create a spirit of fun could only be desirable. TSB Trust Co.'s earlier faith in the festival and the organizers has been rewarded by growth in the scale of the festival and a significant increase in the level and quality of other sponsorship, together with practical support from such authorities as the Hampshire County Council, Southern Arts Association and Southern Tourist Board as well as, of course, Test Valley Borough Council.

TSB Trust Co., as a result of its sponsorship support, has won two awards under the Association for Business Sponsorship of the Arts (ABSA) Business Sponsorship Incentive Scheme.

WINCHESTER AND DISTRICT MACMILLAN NURSE APPEAL

Winchester and District Appeal Committee is very active and successful and TSB Trust Co. supports their aim to raise sufficient funds to meet the costs of two, possibly three, Macmillan nurses whose job is to tend the terminally ill in their own homes.

In addition to ad hoc cash donations, the company's main involvement has been a donation of £10,000 in 1986 in sponsorship of a Fête Champêtre in the grounds of Wherwell Priory, the home of the Countess of Brecknock, DBE, the President of the Winchester and District Committee. The event itself raised £80,000, which was the aim the sponsorship was supporting.

Support for this appeal is continuing into 1988 as the Committee considers the task of raising funds for a Macmillan hospice to be attached to Andover War Memorial Hospital.

CHAPTER 8

MANAGING THE COMMUNICATION
FUNCTION

e~ɔ

GOOD and successful business is the result of giving a number of customers a fair deal – preferably over a long period of time. Both company and customer benefit. Along the line, others – including the employees of the company, the community in which it operates, the shareholders or owners of the company, those who sell on the products or services to the ultimate customer – should also benefit. All this calls for good management by the company and good management means good and effective communication – at all levels and at all times.

This chapter discusses the good management of the communication function, the contribution it makes to the effectiveness of the company's corporate and strategic planning and its implementation. The chapter will identify what is meant by 'the business of communication' and the 'tools of the trade', and will include information and advice to enable the reader to plan a way forward in his or her own business.

The company's corporate plan and communicating it

In setting the company's corporate and business plans, time and consideration will have been given to the long-term development of the organization – and a strategic policy and programme devised and agreed to help ensure that the company is making progress towards its objectives. In the introduction to this book four cornerstones of all communication were defined, making the point that communication is ongoing and not something that happens only as a result of a thought-out campaign, useful though that may be. Communication takes place all the time and that this may be negative in many directions is mostly not anticipated or thought about. This is the hard face of communication and it can adversely affect the company's bottom line. This needs to be recognized by the director dealing with corporate communications and given high priority. Communication is no longer a subject to be relegated to a 'below the salt' position in the company's discussion chambers. It belongs in the boardroom and concerns all levels and tiers of the company.

When a company considers the development of a new product, the introduction of a new service, the building of a new factory or the implementation of a new process, all aspects are considered thoughtfully. Yes, of course, the communication aspects are considered . . . but when, how, and by whom? How much priority are they given and how much in the way of resources? By the time communication is considered as a separate and important area in its own right it is probably too late within the overall planning process, or it may be that communication is given such a low priority by the Board that the resources available in terms of finance and company manpower are totally insufficient.

So, in the company's corporate plan there should be a special section devoted to the communication aspects. Communication has to flow, like water or electricity, and to do so it needs an impetus, a reason, that could be to do with why the customer would want to buy the product, or a shareholder would want to buy the shares of the company, or even why a potential employee wants to work for the company. The purpose of the communication must be clear and apparent in the message. At each stage there will be resistances to be overcome – because most people want to have their existing notions confirmed, not to have any new thoughts added-in.

Setting the priorities

The director has to remember that the company is conducting its business on a public stage. This is true whether it is a small or large organization, private or public. Many different groups of people, ranging from customers to shareholders, politicians to civil servants, journalists to educationists, take, or could take, a lively and legitimate interest in the activities of your organization. For important commercial reasons you should not neglect these wider audiences.

The priority for the director with the remit on corporate communication is to ensure that the company gets its message across and to help the company achieve its overall corporate objectives with maximum support and minimum opposition from the outside world. He must ensure that the company's policies and actions are explained with:

1. Absolute accuracy (of meaning, purpose, facts).
2. Simplicity of language.
3. Brevity.
4. Clarity (no ambiguity).
5. Precision and conciseness.

These are the five 'keys' to good communication. The director must ensure that the company is in tune with legislative and other important and sensitive developments likely to affect its trading policies and products or services and that any resultant requirements are met and monitored as necessary. This process has to be planned to work internally (within the company through all the tiers of the organization) and externally (to all the relevant target audiences of the company). The communications director must be sure that there are adequate resources in terms of finance and time available to get the required message across to the agreed target groups.

In Fig. 8.1 the 'communication circle' is shown. This underlines the importance of the continuous flow of intelligence (market research) through to the planning of communication objectives and programmes, leading to the development of a series of communications projects, their monitoring, and back to the provision of intelligence to be used for future planning. In setting priorities the director should ensure that he can achieve this simple and direct flow.

The tools of communication

The tools are the means of communication, the many different ways in which messages can be planned, researched, studied, presented, conveyed and understood. Thus the communications director will monitor and anticipate political, economic and social developments in areas where the company has or is likely to have a commercial interest. He will also prepare briefing and other material in relation to the company's liaison with political, government, community, and business and industry programmes.

The definition of the company's image and profile and the tracking of this as necessary are also part of the communications director's function. Market research will need to be carried out amongst the general public and more specific groups of opinion-formers and

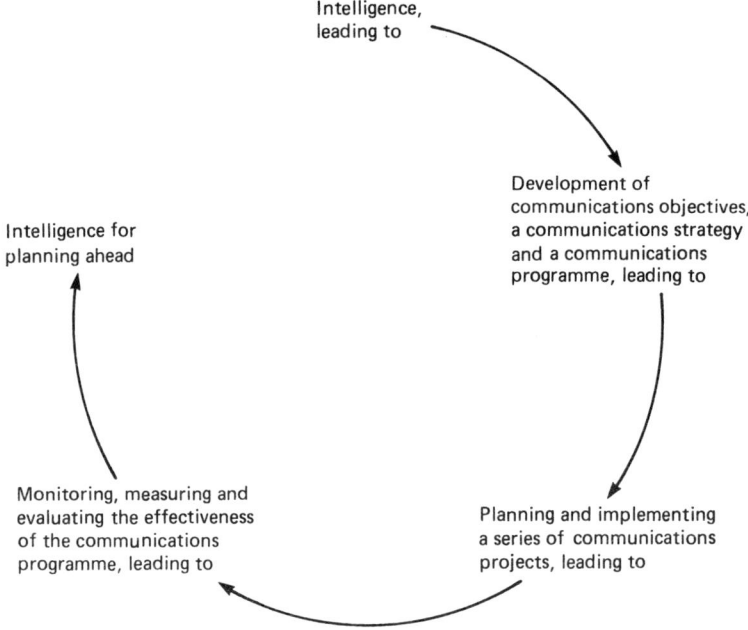

Intelligence,
leading to

Development of
communications objectives,
a communications strategy
and a communications
programme, leading to

Intelligence for
planning ahead

Monitoring, measuring and
evaluating the effectiveness
of the communications
programme, leading to

Planning and implementing
a series of communications
projects, leading to

Fig. 8.1 The communications circle.

pressure groups in order to check how the company is perceived and to plan future presentations. Even in smaller organizations this is still an area which needs attention and resources. The projection of the company's image and profile could well include corporate and financial advertising, especially in the case of larger organizations. In the smaller organization it should be discussed and related specifically to the presentation of the corporate identity, through all the items needing the company livery, from the letterheads to the sales brochures and company vans.

Media relations

The company's media relations are, of course, another key area of operation for the director dealing with corporate communications. They involve handling press enquiries, organizing press conferences, drafting and issuing press releases, arranging for company executives to be interviewed when the occasion arises, arranging for fact-finding tours for journalists and commentators, and ensuring that company officials likely to have contact with the media have had sufficient training. It also involves assessing and evaluating the company record as mentioned in the media and how this is moving forwards or backwards against competitors.

Media relations can play a very active and productive role in the promotion of the company's business. Properly handled with the right level of specialist knowledge and experience, they can help the company to achieve business objectives at modest cost. The policy of the company needs to be as open, clear and explicit as possible. Naturally business confidentiality must be observed, but it is important for company executives not to 'talk down' to journalists, not to 'hide' information, and above all not to answer a media question with the contemptible phrase 'No comment'.

Getting relations with the media right can be a golden asset for any company – large or small. This overall area deserves substantial time and commitment from the director if the company's corporate objectives are to be realized. It is also a pool in which he or she should tread carefully and recognize, realistically, their own level of knowledge and/or expertise. It is perhaps most important of all to recognize any lack of knowledge, skill or experience and if necessary to seek the right level of specialist help – within or outside the organization. (See also Chapter 5, especially tips for dealing with journalists on page 44.)

Events

Events are another area of importance for the director with responsibility for corporate communications. Public and private functions have their place and are very much a part of good business practice. Even modest events, such as the awards for long service to employees, need to be carried out with competence, if not with flair and style. The events schedule for the company should include the proper mix of the following:

1. Major events, which could attract media coverage and/or public, customer or other wide-scale interest.
2. Corporate functions, from the Annual General Meeting to events planned to ensure major customers are made aware of company developments.
3. Business functions, such as seminars and conferences aimed at increasing the levels of knowledge in the company's management and/or workforce.

Trade fairs and exhibitions also have their place in the company's calendar. For the director the decision to attend and participate rests on two factors:

1. Whether the company can afford the overall costs (trade fairs and exhibitions are expensive).
2. Whether or not the company can afford NOT to attend – this is especially relevant if it is known that competitors are to participate.

The cost of hiring exhibition or trade fair spaces is just the start of the costs of participation. They escalate fast, and include:

1. The costs of planning, design and management of the stand itself. This will need to reflect the company's image and message in strong visual terms.
2. Promotion of the company's participation to the relevant target audiences from customers to shareholders.

Literature and visual aids

Well produced corporate literature and visual materials are a further and important area for the director's attention. These range from the annual report, the employees' and/or shareholders' annual reports, to special reports on specific issues and company corporate and sales brochures, catalogues or guidance and practice notes. These are today considered essential for the credibility of a company seeking to make good progress in the competitive business world. Again, it is likely that the director may feel that he or she is already very familiar with the preparation of corporate literature and similar aids to business, but is he? There is an enormous variation between the excellent, the simply good, the mediocre and woefully bad in this field, and the result of being on the lower end of the scale in the mind of the recipient of your company's brochure or film will most probably directly affect the company's bottom line.

Again it is vital to know whether you, and those working with you, are good enough for the job. If you need specialist, experienced help much your cheapest option is to recognize that and to get it. Remember, though, that spending large amounts of money will not necessarily ensure that you get the right results. In fact, very often the more important the creative concept developed to achieve your objective the more reasonable in execution the project could turn out to be.

In this area the director should be looking at the following:

1. Special projects, such as awards, studies, special briefings to groups from MPs to environmentalists.
2. Booklets, brochures and other printed material.
3. Films, for distribution to both general and specialist audiences.
4. Video and audio tapes for use for promotions, public relations, education, sales or training purposes.
5. Photographic services to cover company events and other agreed subjects.
6. Making available company material as necessary to media, distributors and libraries specially selected as being relevant.

Staff newspapers and in-house or external journals are another aspect of communications for the director to consider. These are seen as being of increasing importance in an age of instant communication. The director must also consider the production of briefing newssheets on selected issues for the relevant tiers of management. Speech notes and speech/lecture aids for directors and other key executives may be necessary so that they can take advantage of opportunities to promote the company's philosophy, practices and products or services on relevant trade and industry and/or public platforms.

Participation in the community

Participation in wider community responsibility areas might range from donations and special project work with selected charities to funding special areas of research. Increasingly in this area, too, companies are being asked to be 'a good corporate citizen'. Some possible fields of action might be as follows:

1. Community-based initiatives helping to create new jobs and tackle the social issues of the day.
2. Local community projects.
3. Educational liaison and related services.
4. Charity and arts sponsorship and projects.

The case study on the TSB Trust Company in Andover is useful in this context (page 79).

Communication as a marketing tool

Communication is clearly a powerful and effective aspect of marketing. The use of market research, other elements of the marketing mix, to include specialist and consumer display advertising, have already found their places in the many books devoted to those subjects. Suffice to say here that all the elements in the marketing and sales campaigns of the company should be fused with the corporate communications programme. In organizational terms this calls for the following:

1. Identifying those with responsibility in this area.
2. Agreeing the methods and criteria for monitoring action and progress.
3. Implementing the means of co-ordination through a structure of meetings, reports, etc.

This is essential to ensure that those receiving all the communications of the company are receiving properly co-ordinated messages so that the sum total of the whole exceeds by far the sum of the individual messages.

It is appropriate, however, to say a few words about the importance of 'image' in corporate communications work. Wally Olins, the distinguished corporate 'image-maker', says:

> In the old days, some products were good, some were bad, some were expensive and some were cheap, so it was relatively easy to make a choice. Nowadays, though, all the people who make lousy products are out of business, so there are only good products left. In any field you like to mention – banking, potato crisps, civil aircraft, power stations – you won't find much difference between the competing products or services available. They will all be good, they will all be reliable and, give or take a bit, they will all be the same price.
>
> So, if we can't make a choice on a rational basis, we have to make a choice for emotional reasons.
>
> Never underestimate the importance of emotion in our lives. After all, most of us make the most important decision of our lives – who we marry – for emotional reasons. So, increasingly, when we have to make the choice between competing products or services, we make the choice emotionally because rational factors no longer count.
>
> What it all boils down to is reputation. We don't buy things we haven't heard of, but we do buy things whose reputation for one reason or another appeals to us.
>
> A company acquires a reputation through communication – what it communicates, how it communicates, how much and to whom. Communication comes from employees, through rumour, myth, pieces in newspapers and on television, as well as through brochures and advertising.
>
> In today's world, communication is all.

Picking the right people to communicate

It is important for the director to know how good, bad or indifferent he and his team may be at communication, and if necessary, they should seek experience and talented help from outside the company. Within the company sensitivities and hackles may rise and it may be said that a particular person is going for 'personal publicity'. This is nonsense, for if a company has the good fortune to have on its staff a natural and talented communicator that is a great asset. It would be as great a folly not to use that asset to the full as it would be to buy an expensive piece of capital equipment and to use it only for half an hour a day!

What mix of talents are important for success?

1. The director should have a wide appreciation of the outside world and a sensitivity to key opportunities, and problems. A sense of timing is important and substantial resources of persuasiveness, vision and logic are also very useful so that he or she can get colleagues to understand why planning, finance and action are needed.

2. The director needs to be able to pick a new breed of people to help with the work, who can understand, manage and release the potential in communication. In the 'in-house' team a variety of talents are needed – creative talents, administrative talents (the ability to plan, implement and budget) and communication skills (getting to know and get on with people).

In-house or out-of-house?

It is simpler and most cost-effective for a company to have its corporate communications run by its own staff so that it can be managed with the right level of confidentiality. Depending on the level of talent, experience and ability within the organization, outside specialists may (indeed probably will) be needed. These come in many different types and varieties and can be used for many different purposes. They range from market research specialists, image-makers, advertising agencies, public relations consultancies, specialist mailing and other houses. Their services are explored in Chapters 4 and 5.

In deciding to involve an outside agency, such as a public relations consultancy, it is useful to know something about how they calculate their fees. There are several different systems used. One popular method is as follows:

1. The programme of work is assessed.
2. The amount of time involved from staff at different levels of responsibility within their organization is worked out.
3. The time is then costed, bearing in mind the employment costs of the persons involved.
4. The consultancy's 'multiplier factor' is applied which could involve multiplying the overall cost of the time to operate the campaign by between 2.4 and 4 times to allow for the costs of the back-up services, overheads, profit margins etc.

Essentially, you are buying time within the consultancy; it is up to you to determine just how much of that time you are wasting. If you call for over-detailed documentation, more administration and reporting procedures than you need, unnecessary meetings, etc., then you will be adding to your own bills. (See also Chapter 4 on using a consultancy and Appendix 1 for tips on how to select a consultancy and how to be a good client).

Managing the corporate communication function and ensuring that it works to the benefit of the company is well worth doing – and worth doing well. It repays attention to detail. The image and the reality of the company are at one with each other. Robert Worcester, Chairman of MORI, market and opinion researchers, comments:

> Corporate image is important, and benefits do accrue to well-conceived, well-organized and effectively-presented corporate communications programmes. It is important for the corporate communications programme to have the support of senior management; to be communicated to the workforce, so that it can put its powerful muscle behind it; to ensure that shareholders' goodwill can be tapped and that the other publics of importance can see a co-ordinated effort.
>
> Images improve as slowly as glaciers move, but can be destroyed overnight. As one observer put it, 'The building of a corporate image is like planting asparagus – you should have started three years ago'.

Summary

Communication is as important a function in an organization as the development and introduction of the company's products or services, as the factories or plants, or as a new process. It is, in effect, the 'other half of the apple'. The correct priority given to the area of communication – together with the necessary resources – could well provide a most valuable investment for the company. Knowing the company's current capability in the area of communication is very important.

   This chapter examines the elements of good management of the communication function, identifying priorities of the 'business' of communication and how it could contribute to the overall strategic objectives of the company. The importance of setting priorities and recognizing the different 'tools' of the communications business are underlined with the five 'keys' of good communication and the continuous flow of communication. The importance of image in corporate communications work is considered and the type of talents needed to ensure good management of the communication function in a company. The priorities for picking outside specialists where required are examined how best to use such services. A director of corporate communications must be a 'good listener' and ensure two-way communications.

CHAPTER 9

VALUE FOR MONEY IN
CORPORATE COMMUNICATIONS

ℰ✍❀

Communications practice within companies

How can we evaluate and measure results so as to decide whether or not they represent value for money – and make sure that they do?

To answer these questions a questionnaire was sent to the 50 fastest growing private companies in the United Kingdom and also to the 50 top public companies. This was achieved through co-operation with *The Growth Companies Register*, a leading authority on Britain's fastest growing private companies. The 50 top public companies were those identified as such by *The Financial Times*. The response to the two studies was interesting.

The fifty fastest growing private companies

As can be easily imagined, some of these companies were very small and some very new. Communication as such was, it was suspected, a fairly unknown and uncharted sea for some of them. Possibly the thought of operating a corporate communications programme would be a new concept. Indeed only eight answers were received from these questionnaires. They included some comments to the effect that 'the reason we are a "fastest growing company" is because we don't waste time answering questionnaires such as yours! (Incidentally, what is this book you are talking about, and where can we get it, how much does it cost and could you send us a free copy?)'[1]

Almost without exception results indicated that little thought was given or effort made in the area of monitoring or measuring the results from communication campaigns; indeed it appeared that there was little evidence that such campaigns were planned. If they were, planning was basic.

The fifty top public companies

Perhaps understandably there were more respondents in this area. In all 18 forms were returned. In this area, too, we received one or two choice comments – perhaps surprisingly indicating that the request for such information was unusual and that there were no current practices to report! Equally surprising was the fact that there was no response at all from at least three companies with reputations for effective corporate communications. (The forms were issued twice so it is unlikely that they were not received.)

The results of the study indicated that the responsibility for the function of corporate communication is given to many different types and levels of executive in both public and private companies, ranging from the company secretary to the public relations or marketing manager.

Responses to the questionnaires might be summarized as follows:

1. The need for evaluation was accepted unanimously.
2. The need for the use of outside specialists was generally accepted. This use related to particular responsibilities. The company's outside consultancy seemed to be given the responsibility for the evaluation process more often than we would have expected – thus making the consultancy judge and jury in their own case!
3. All relevant respondents evaluated communication programmes related to fast moving consumer goods, but frequency of this exercise varied, however.
4. All respondents evaluated company image and how this was moving.
5. Issues were evaluated ('quite often' by seven respondents, 'sometimes' by three, 'rarely' by two).
6. Subscriptions to databases tracking and quantifying elements of social change were popular.
7. Traditional methods of monitoring performance were used. Included in these were media monitoring, Hansard, press releases, opinion-former meetings, omnibus market research. Edited data was used in the majority of cases.

8. Fifty per cent of respondents identified evaluation as a separate cost area, but of those 50 per cent the proportion of overall project budget (excluding overheads) generally allocated to evaluation differed widely. The highest figure quoted was 10 per cent and the lowest 2 per cent. It must be remembered, however, that the type of organization involved varied enormously – from large industrial group to manufacturer of fast moving consumer goods.

9. The most popular method of evaluation indicated was the use of market research polls annually (and even more frequently) to track image, externally, with Members of Parliament, industry leaders, financial journalists, employees etc.

10. Advertising campaigns were the subject of frequent evaluation studies.

Conclusions drawn from both these studies would indicate a need for a focus to be given to the whole area of measurement and evaluation, with more consistency in terms of the executive in the company charged with this responsibility. The subject is one which would benefit from wider debate towards the setting of guidelines which, in time, could be recognized as authoritative and so of practical reference and use to the company.

Monitoring the programme

An essential first step in corporate marketing is a clear definition of the audiences which a programme is to reach. The widest corporate communication programmes are designed for very broad audiences – the public, employees, customers, opinion-formers, government and various City groups – whilst the narrowest may only be aimed at a small range of targets, such as brokers and analysts perhaps.

If the programme's objective is to raise awareness amongst the general public, then a simple quantitative measure is usually taken. Omnibus surveys – showing the extent to which recognition of the company's name has changed, for example – are useful and economical, since they enable a client to buy one or more questions on a continuing survey.

If the target audience is City analysts and the aim of the campaign is to change attitudes towards a company of which they are already well aware, then this type of basic survey would clearly be insufficient. To obtain fuller information, the research would need to be qualitative in nature as well as quantitative – less about absolute numbers and more about the relative balance of positive and negative attitudes.

Whichever approach is selected, it is vital for monitoring to be included as a structured part of the overall communication programme. Research should indeed be the starting point for the design of any strategy, providing the following are taken into account:

1. An initial reference point indicating the level of awareness of the company concerned.
2. A sampling of the attitudes towards the company.
3. An identification of competitor's attitudes towards the company and the quality of their communication efforts.
4. An identification of the target group's media patterns, to aid the most effective media selection.

This initial survey (a benchmark study, see also Chapter 3) will, therefore, give clear information aiding detailed planning of the strategy, whilst at the same time providing a benchmark of the existing state of opinion against which changes occurring as a result of the communications programme can be measured.

In addition to the wealth of knowledge which can be gained at this stage, timed replication of the research is valuable. The frequency of replication is a function of the intensity of a campaign, since the heavier a campaign, the more likely the occurrence of a significant shift in opinion. For example, a corporate advertising campaign backed by heavy bursts of TV advertising may require monitoring as frequently as every three to four months. A lower-key communications programme which consists of an annual report and brokers' lunch programme may only need to be surveyed every year or 18 months because corporate image would move very slowly under these circumstances. What is essential is that tracking occurs regularly and as an integrated element in the overall strategy.

The benefits of replication are that it allows the following:

1. Measurement of the absolute success of a campaign.
2. Analysis of its success in conveying specific messages.
3. A comparative and continuous measure of corporate image vis-à-vis the competition.
4. An update of the information gathered in the benchmark study.

Through replication, research interacts to ensure that a programme continues to be relevant to the target market and hence maximizes the opportunities available. Without it there is no guarantee six months or a year into a programme either that it is succeeding, or that the messages which it is seeking to deliver are still applicable to the current market situation; or indeed that the cost of the campaign has been money well spent.[2]

Working with communications specialists

Looking at the subject from the point of view of the company or organization concerned, the models available for study appear to be few and far between. Some companies do, however, follow procedures to assess the performance of their in-house team and/or consultancies operating for them. Here as an example is a distillation of how leading companies would evaluate communication consultancy work:

1. Performance objectives would be listed – these would have been agreed by both consultancy and client at the beginning of the reporting period. If formal objectives had not been set, the reasons for this would be set out.
2. The reporting period would be agreed between consultancy and client – three months, six months or annually.
3. The client company would identify the strengths and weaknesses of performance in the consultancy – related to the achievement of the objectives.
4. The company would identify whether or not the consultancy had taken the initiative. Several different areas of the operation involved would be listed. The company would indicate whether or not the consultancy's understanding of or interest in key business issues facing the company was up to expectation.
5. The company would identify any major problems which existed in the consultancy/client relationship and would seek to be fair in indicating whether client-related factors contributed to consultancy problems.
6. The company would assess whether the consultancy's overall performance during any particular reporting period was better or worse than the previous period and any reasons for this.
7. The company would identify any need to improve or enhance the relationship over the coming period (six or 12 months).
8. The company would make an evaluation of the account management in the consultancy. This would relate to several criteria, which would be graded, and reasons for the grades awarded would be identified. Such criteria would include:

(a) ethical and professional standards;
(b) quality of planning;
(c) ability to achieve objectives;
(d) competence of staff, frequency of change/replacement;
(e) contribution to helping to achieve business goals;
(f) understanding of the nature of business of the company;
(g) commitment to and involvement with the business;
(h) quality of thinking and initiative;
(i) responsiveness;
(j) reporting systems;
(k) effectiveness of planning and execution of the specific campaigns.

9. The company would make an evaluation of financial and administrative services. It would need reports on the billing and accounting procedures, effective estimating and control of costs. An important issue to be noted would be cost consciousness (ability to keep within budgets, proof of care about client's money and similar factors).

10. The analysis by the company would include details of any retainers paid, bases for fees and expenses for ad hoc activities – with hourly or daily rates identified as well as total remuneration for the year, listed by fees and expenses for each project. The company would expect to see reports and time sheets relevant to the specific programme of activity.

How far can evaluation go?

In time there will be further accepted procedures and guidance on the matter of evaluation and measurement of communication programmes, to go alongside the necessary research and tracking of campaign performance. In certain areas, such as advertising, measurement techniques already exist, but it would be agreed that even they are as yet imperfect. It is not beyond possibility that, in time, a communications standard will be created against which measurement can be made. At a time when information technology is an explosive force in the communications industry it is difficult to keep abreast of all the techniques which may be available, now and in the future. Organizations which are innovating in this area are justifiably keen to keep their techniques to themselves until they are proved beyond reasonable doubt.

The following is a summary of the priorities for the director to bear in mind when evaluating programmes:

1. Budget – ensure the completion of activity within the agreed budget and timescale.
2. Awareness – define and agree an increase in the knowledge of the organization amongst the defined audience.
3. Attitude – establish whether or not there has been a shift in opinion about the organization.
4. Media – review the level and tone of news and other coverage during specific agreed periods.
5. Position – decide where the company stands in the market against its competitors.
6. Response – calculate the number of enquiries and/or leads generated by the campaign.
7. Share price – establish the value that the investor puts upon the company.
8. Sales – establish any changes in sales volumes or prices that can be related to the campaign alone.[3]

A large return for investment in corporate communications

The two case histories on page 107 at the end of this chapter are examples of investment in corporate communication being amply rewarded and where the return has been immeasurably more than the investment itself.

The first concerns Stanley Tools where, over many years, a modest investment in education built up a bank of goodwill with the educationists worth its weight in gold. During the ten years to 1987, while the United Kingdom went through a period of inflation and recession, the company initiated a series of Stanley Lectures with the objective of underlining the significance of craft, design and technology in education. This 'Decade of Stanley Lectures' and the company's commitment to education at a time when other major manufacturers were reducing their expenditure in this area, further consolidated Stanley's position in the educational arena. It is considerably to the company's credit that the subject area of craft, design and technology is no longer a 'second class citizen' in the school curriculum and the company's contribution to the increased recognition and resources given to the subject is recognized widely.

The second case history concerns Gieves & Hawkes, for more than 200 years a living legend, naval and military tailors to the great and the good. The company wished to raise its profile internationally and was seeking a major development in international markets. At the time of the wedding of the future Duke and Duchess of York in July 1986 the company inaugurated a 'Dress and Protocol Advisory Service' for use by members of the public in the month before the Royal Wedding. In association with Debrett's Peerage the service was launched on 26 June 1986 at an exhibition illustrating the long association of the two companies with Royalty. This was opened by Robert Gieve, a fifth generation member of the founding family of Gieves & Hawkes. Media exposure was instantaneous and international. Television coverage included the United States, Japan, Australia and other areas important to the future plans of the company. Press coverage was comprehensive. Whilst comparisons with advertising media costs are invidious it is clear that the exposure given to the company's services and activities was worth millions of pounds.

Why things go wrong

What happens if something goes wrong? Even more important, what can be done about it? Where can the director turn for help and advice – even for redress?

In-house department

This area is very much under the control of the organization itself and the director should already have a very good idea of particular strengths and weaknesses. If the organization is a large one, however, it is likely that the director may not have a detailed picture. It is important, therefore, that he or she reviews the priority given to the area of corporate communications and considers the company's requirement in relation to the number and quality of staff employed by the department. It is essential that, as for any director, the person leading a department responsible to the Board for corporate communications should have the right style of intellect and experience for the job.

Frequently, with in-house departments, there is no annual plan against which the in-house team should perform. Special campaigns and specific projects, too, may be subject to less detailed scrutiny than would be the case if an outside organization had been involved. The company corporate plan should, however, specifically include this detailed scrutiny.

The director should, therefore, review the reasons why things have gone wrong. These should include:

1. Inadequate planning, co-ordination and supervision.
2. Inadequate ability and experience in the in-house team. (Key executives should be members of appropriate professional bodies to ensure their competence and ethical standards.)
3. Inadequate consideration of the viability or otherwise of the particular programme at the time a 'go ahead' decision was taken.
4. Personal problems of staff inhibiting performance.

It is possible that nothing can be done to contain damage already experienced. Before deciding this, however, the company should consider the following points:

1. Were outside specialists involved? If so, was the problem in any way related to the input to them or to their lack of performance?
2. What specific moves can be taken by the organization to repair the damage and to preclude a similar experience in future?
3. How should the nature or training of the in-house team be changed in order to prevent such an occurrence happening again?

Outside suppliers of services

It is very likely that the company will already have relationships with many outside suppliers of the services that go to make up corporate communications. Such suppliers can include advertising agencies, public relations consultancies, market research organizations, specialist sales promotion houses, design consultancies, and even print, film and video companies.

It is important for the director to check that a service organization is a member of the appropriate accredited trade association or professional body. This will go a long way towards ensuring that the persons dealing with the company's affairs are competent and are working to the codes of practice which operate in the particular area. (Details of some important codes of practice can be found in Appendix 8 on page 144.)

If the director has recently taken up responsibility for corporate communications he or she should review current and projected specialist suppliers with a view to checking the following:

1. Professional reputation of the service organization.
2. Professional qualifications, reputations and standards of competence of executives involved in working on the company's business, also their stability in terms of length of service.

3. Track record of the organization – with particular reference to how long their clients stay with them – a useful indicator on the stability of the business and standard of service to clients.
4. Also important in today's changing world is to know if the organization has been recently subject to a takeover or is likely to be in this position in the near future, as this could have an effect on the level of efficiency and motivation of staff.
5. Endorsements of the organization and its key staff working on the company's business.

(See also checklist on selecting an outside consultancy in Appendix 1 on page 118.)

How to complain

If things have gone wrong and a director believes that the company has not received value for money from an outside consultancy, what are the avenues for repairing the damage and redress?

This is a difficult area and as yet avenues for complaint and redress are not as fully developed as in most other categories of commerce and industry. Here, however, is a step-by-step guide to processing a complaint on corporate communication:

Step 1

The director should ensure that the company has prepared an accurate written analysis of what happened and why, with documentation. There should be a clear statement of the results hoped for following the complaint (in order of priority, as some reconciliation or compromise may be necessary).

Step 2

A meeting with the outside organization should be called. It is best to contact the chief executive by name for this purpose.

Step 3

If the company has not been able to reach a satisfactory conclusion with the outside organization, the director should contact the relevant trade association or professional body. He or she should first find out the name of the chief executive or official concerned and the nature of the complaints mechanism the association or institute operates. A meeting with the chief executive of the organization or the relevant official should be requested to seek help and advice, with a further meeting planned to take place in due course with the disciplinary committee of the body. Before this time the director should be familiar with the track record and procedure of complaints handling of the particular trade association or professional body. He or she will then be in a position to predict the likely outcome and to negotiate accordingly.

The director should prepare the case carefully and present it with accuracy and clarity. He or she should indicate the support of his whole Board for the action taken and their resolve to achieve an outcome satisfactory to both sides.

Step 4

If the matter is still unresolved the director has the following options to consider:

1. The publicity sanction – frequently a powerful one. This should be used with care and an alert eye on legal implications.
2. The legal sanction – here the director will need to keep a careful eye on the likely levels and escalations of cost!
3. Taking the matter up with government departments and other relevant bodies who may be interested in the particular case.

Summary

Value for money in corporate communications is difficult to assess and assessment needs resources of time and finance. It is important to know the levels of competence and ethics available to the company in an in-house department or through specialist outside agencies. If something goes wrong it is important to act quickly, logically and legally. To achieve a result satisfactory to both sides reconciliation and realistic compromise will probably be effective. Future problems can be minimized by checking up carefully on the type of person (and their professional qualifications and ethical standards) entrusted with responsibility for planning and/or implementing programmes of corporate communication. In particular, if outside specialists are involved their stability in employment is a key factor.

This chapter describes the basic technique of monitoring a programme of corporate communications and suggests some ways of assessing the work of a public relations department or consultancy. It concludes with a description of how to handle a situation in which a company's corporate communication programme is not performing well. It indicates a range of remedial option.

References

1. *Fifty Fastest Growing Private Companies* (Financial Publishing Ltd, 31–37 Cursitor Street, London EC4A 1LT).
2. Valin Pollen's contribution to this analysis is acknowledged.
3. Roger Haywood's contribution to this check-list is acknowledged.

Case Study 1
COMMUNICATING THROUGH EDUCATION – THE STANLEY LECTURE

Stanley Tools

Consultancy
Cadogan Management Ltd.

Dates
1977 to 1987

Summary
Stanley Tools is the largest woodworking handtool manufacturer in Europe. At a time of recession and when the manufacturing industry in the United Kingdom was hard hit, the company elected to confirm its support for education through the introduction of a series of Stanley Lectures, the tenth lecture being delivered in mid October 1987.

Opportunity
The subject of craft, design and technology in the mid 1970s was still in its infancy and its full potential for helping to develop a child's character had yet to be realized. Through their close co-operation with the educational profession over the years Stanley Tools was able to plan this unusual initiative.

Strategy

The importance of proper recognition for the subject area of craft, design and technology was accepted by senior educationists in the United Kingdom. Stanley Tools had an active involvement in this area with the operation of its Education Service providing educational lectures, lecture aids and educational literature to schools over the years. In addition, for many years, Stanley Tools had published and distributed an educational publication, *The Stanley Link in Craft Design and Technology*. This publication had focused on the intellectual arguments for giving greater priority to technology and related education. It was respected by educationists internationally and its columns were quoted on numerous occasions. Thus the company was encouraged by educationists to introduce a complementary project to reinforce the overall educational effort of the company – and to project the company's corporate profile and social responsibility in so doing.

The Stanley Lecture was planned with the active help and co-operation of an educational panel. This group of distinguished educationists, also representing the educational authorities, decided both the theme of each lecture and the identity of the lecturer/s and chairmen. The venue for the Stanley Lecture was the Royal Society of Arts in London. Invitation lists were drawn up with the help of the educational panel and reflected the theme of each lecture. The invited audience included distinguished figures from the world of education, also from industry, trade unions and the media. Each lecture was printed and requests for copies ran into thousands.

For each lecture there was a waiting list as the reputation of the Stanley Lecture became known and an invitation to attend became considered a status symbol of a distinguished and dedicated educationist. Names of the chairmen and lecturers reflected 'the great and the good' – and included the Duke of Gloucester, Sir Patrick Nuttgens, Sir Monty Finniston, Sir Alex Smith, John Swain (HMI), Denis Lawton, and Tom Dodd (MSC and previously on the hugely successful and popular Technical and Vocational Education Initiative (TVEI) project).

Results

A decade of Stanley Lectures has made its mark on the subject area of craft, design and technology. It is intended that they should now be published in book form and will thus bear evidence to the fact that, when things in Britain were difficult for a major manufacturer grappling with changing international markets, the will was there to support the new generation and to enable the country to build a better future based on better technological education for the country's children. The Stanley contribution is acknowledged widely and the reputation of the company and its corporate identity have been enhanced by this evidence of the company's concern for wider priorities at an important and difficult time.

Case Study 2
RAISING A COMPANY'S PROFILE – with international emphasis

Gieves & Hawkes

Consultancy
Cadogan Management Ltd.

Dates
Spring/summer 1986.

Summary
Gieves & Hawkes, founded as a naval and military tailors in 1785, requested Cadogan Management Ltd to put forward proposals for a publicity campaign to increase awareness of the Gieves & Hawkes name.

Opportunity
Cadogan Management Ltd identified the following opportunities:

1. To increase awareness of the Gieves & Hawkes name.
2. To underline the company as an authority on matters sartorial, both civilian and military, and as arbiters of taste and style.

3. To identify the company's long association with pageantry and Royal ceremonial for which Britain is famous.

Strategy

Cadogan Management Ltd proposed that Gieves & Hawkes, in association with Debrett's Peerage, should launch a Dress and Protocol Advisory Service for use by members of the public in the month before the wedding of the future Duke and Duchess of York in 1986. The combination of Gieves & Hawkes' experience of naval and military dress and etiquette, and of correct civilian dress, would be matched by the expertise of Debretts in correct form and manner.

Programme

1. A formal invitation was issued. (One important aspect of the programme was to ensure that all invitations and published material were socially and sartorially correct in every detail.)
2. The Advisory Service was launched on 26 June 1986. An exhibition illustrating the long association of Debretts and Gieves and Hawkes with Royalty was opened by Robert Gieve, Vice-Chairman of Gieves & Hawkes and a fifth generation member of the founding family.
3. A press pack was issued which included a history of the company's naval traditions and long outfitting service to the Royal Navy, plus details of uniforms and the observance of protocol on Royal occasions.
4. A telephone advisory service hotline was implemented. Experts handled enquiries on sartorial matters as well as etiquette.
5. The Royal Wedding. Only on the day of the Wedding, 26 July 1986, did Gieves & Hawkes announce, with full colour illustrations, that they had made the uniforms for the pages at the wedding.
6. All the pages received from Robert Gieve the equivalent one day's pay appropriate to their rank in the original coinage of the year represented by their uniforms – the 'midshipmen' each got a silver sixpence and the 'sailors' received a silver groat.

Results

1. The press launch was attended by seven camera crews from news and royal wedding teams from around the world and by 50 newspaper and magazine journalists.
2. The media coverage given was afterwards assessed as totalling some £3 million worth of comparable advertising costs, with television in Australia, America, Japan, France, Italy, the United Kingdom and many other countries; many radio interviews around the world, including New Zealand; and international newspaper coverage.
3. The provision of the telephone hotline provided an on-going story for the media to follow up.
4. When it emerged that Gieves & Hawkes had made the pages' uniforms, awareness already created ensured further television, radio and newspaper coverage.
5. The authority of Gieves & Hawkes as arbiters of good taste and style was underlined.
6. The profile of the company was greatly enhanced – to such an extent that the marketing director of the company received many letters from PR agencies offering their future services!

CHAPTER 10

THE END RESULT –
CONSUMER AFFAIRS

❧

At the end of the day, the results of any programme of corporate communications are directly expressed as the economic health and prosperity of the company. The link between good communications and good financial results is most direct and striking in the field of consumer affairs. Consumer affairs is an important and growing component of corporate communications. It is in the increasing dialogues with the consumers of goods and services (the customers) that companies are able to judge and monitor their performance in the area of corporate communications.

Customer complaints

There is a growing awareness that customers are important. The whole area of customer liaison, complaints handling and consumer affairs is coming into its own. In the United States, for example, there are now organizations specializing in techniques to convert customer complaints into lucrative new business for the company. Complaints handling done well is a proven contributor to increased profits. Surprisingly perhaps, customers who have complained and been treated well increase their brand and other loyalty to a company.

In the United Kingdom, however, how many have heard of 'that square peg in the round hole', the customer complaints officer, the executive who is shuffled from pillar to post, only in the end to be shuffled – indeed almost shut – into a little office and given the complaints file to cope with. Alas, only too frequently he or she becomes almost a recluse. Members of the company related to the marketing function may find this person 'depressing'. They are reluctant to admit that there could be customers critical of the company's products or services. Often, too, when the customer complaints officer has moved on (or even out of the company) drawers full of unanswered complaints letters have been found. Yet this is an important company function – too often given a low level of priority and/or resource.

That the customer who complains is a good, fast, cheap and valid route to research information for a company is now achieving recognition. And the broader area of consumer affairs is now coming into its own. Initial recognition of the importance of customer relations came from the United States, with the formation of the Society of Consumer Affairs Professionals in Business (SOCAP), now some 1500 members strong. SOCAP was formed in 1973 and became established in the United Kingdom in 1986. SOCAP UK now has over 100 members – the list of their organizations indeed constitutes a register of companies practising good corporate communications programmes.

The customer relations function

What is the customer relations function? Defined by Jan Walsh who chairs SOCAP UK, it is, 'The application of a series of professional disciplines which underpin the commercial effort of the enterprise by helping to harness and maintain customer loyalty.' This sentiment is echoed, and taken further, with the addition of a note of warning by Ron Zemke and Karl Albrecht of Service America. They say, 'Customer loyalty is, at best, circumstantial, fragile and fleeting – it fades as service declines.' As Jan Walsh says, 'the excellence of a company is crucially dependent on it having an harmonious relationship with a loyal customer base. The challenge in today's economic, social and business environment is to make use of the customers' experience to the customers' own advantage.

'The customer relations function, therefore, impinges on all aspects of business but, in particular, on the commercial relationship between a member of staff and the customer. Customer relations is so closely related to brand and company loyalty that it is perhaps surprising that it has taken so long for companies to recognize the connection between the customer who complains today and the company's bottom line tomorrow.

'Every business has customers, of course, persons or businesses that use their services, but they can be of very different types. Some customers are external to the enterprise and this is what is normally understood by the term 'customer'. Others are colleagues, 'internal customers'. The customer relations function ensures that all staff develop positive relationships with their internal customers and that this ethos permeates their behaviour towards their external customers.

'All too often customer relations initiatives are ad hoc and unrelated either to the fundamental objectives of the company or to each other. The position of the customer relations department within an organization is also an important factor – ideally it should form part of the marketing function and be an ingredient in the marketing mix. It is increasingly seen as a priority area for regular review at Board level.'

A good customer relations programme

How can a company implement a programme of good customer relations? Here are some illustrations:

1. Superquinn Ltd is a chain of supermarkets in the Republic of Ireland where commitment to the customer starts right at the top, with the managing director, Feargal Quinn. Managing the customers' experience is made easier by the involvement of consumer panels who meet regularly to discuss issues of customer concern. Feargal Quinn himself attends almost all these meetings and responds directly to customers, either by implementing suggestions made by the panel, or by explaining how company decisions are reached.

2. Listening to the company's customers, spotlighting issues and responding to customer concerns are the reason for the establishment of British Telecom's consumer liaison panels in 1984 – the first company in the United Kingdom to do so. Since those early experiments in company/customer communication, the panels now have their own database on Prestel, electronic reference library and regular communications using the latest technology. It will be recognized that it takes time to pull through a substantial change in customer attitudes to a large organization. Some of the innovations resulting from this initiative from British Telecom still require time before their effects are fully seen.

Other models of consumer or customer liaison panels are appearing in organizations of many types and levels of operation in the United Kingdom.

Relations with opinion-formers

Those familiar with corporate communication programmes will be aware of the importance of the correct dialogue with the 'opinion-formers', such as the spokesmen for consumer organizations. Yet, despite legislation, including the 1986 Financial Services Act, which shows that governments listen closely to what consumer affairs specialists and consumer organizations are saying to them, business is all too often inept and clumsy in its programmes of communication and liaison with such groups.

In the world of consumer affairs the director of corporate communications must consider liaison with, in the United Kingdom, organizations such as the Office of Fair Trading, the Institute of Trading Standards Administration and the National Consumer Council at one end, and consumer groups such as the Consumers' Association, the National Federation of Consumer Groups, and the women's organizations, such as the National Federation of Women's Institutes and the National Association of Women's Clubs at the other. The director should understand how advice agencies such as the National Association of Citizens Advice Bureaux work. Environmentalists (of whom there are now over three million in the United Kingdom), the 'green' organizations such as Friends of the Earth and the Soil Association and environmental charities such as the Conservation Foundation must all be considered by those concerned with corporate communications.

The right company image

David Bernstein, Chairman of the Creative Business, is one of the most respected figures in the advertising industry and an authority on corporate communication. He believes that detailed self-examination is an important first step to successful communication; and that no corporate activity can be undertaken until a company has defined precisely what it believes in (philosophy) and what sort of company it is (personality). Their physical expression is the identity and the result is the image – the way the company is perceived. His book on the subject, *Image and Reality*,[1] stresses the need for companies to recognize the central importance of effective and accurate corporate communication to their mainstream business. He also believes a certain visionary quality is needed to recognize fully the importance of the communications task – as far as anyone outside the company is concerned, a company's image is its reality. He says,

> What else does an observer have to judge it by other than its products and its image? Image affects choice of product, of partner, of whether to work for a

company – something with that power must be real. It is important for us, therefore, to try to ensure that responsibility for it is upheld at the highest level.

David Bernstein has been preaching the gospel of good corporate communication for years – underlining also his view that the company which communicates well *internally* has fewer problems externally. This vision is now a reality in many companies. The numbers of those who recognize and practise the principles of good corporate communication are growing, and may be found in small as well as large companies.

Suppliers of communications services may be found in city and country. The explosion in information technology has harnessed and made available talents and facilities to all businesses, big and small. Access to good design is instantly available and the recognition of its value is growing.

Every company is already deeply involved in corporate communications of some kind; it is up to the director to ensure that it does not benefit competitors at the expense of his company, but rather that it all works well for the development of his company's business.

Summary

Consumer affairs have been neglected until quite recently. It is now, however, becoming recognized as a central element in corporate strategy. Consumer affairs is rapidly developing, and forms a fitting conclusion to this book about making corporate communication effective and profitable.

Reference

1. David Bernstein, *Image and Reality* (Holt Rinehart Winston/The Advertising Association, 1984).

APPENDICES

❧

For the busy director, in an age of information technology, there is arguably too much information available. The problem often is to sift through this when an urgent need makes itself felt. These appendices, therefore, list a few (only) useful organizations, media and services which the reader may need to access at short notice.

MAKING USE OF
EXTERNAL CONSULTANCIES

இ❦ெ

Selecting an outside consultancy

Check up on the consultancy's reputation and competence, whether it be advertising, public relations or market research and ensure you have the following information:

On the organization itself

1. How long established.
2. Size – people/turnover.
3. Growth pattern.
4. Client stability.
5. Types of business handled.
6. Experience in your area.
7. List and qualifications of staff – full-time, part-time.
8. Staff to be assigned to your business – qualifications, length of service.
9. Percentage of time to be devoted to your business in relation to contract.
10. Staff turnover over past three years.
11. Reporting approval and accounting procedures.

On their clients

1. Client list – current and past.
2. Oldest clients – length of service.
3. Average length of client/company relationship.
4. Specific client endorsements.

Above all – ensure you know the answers to the following:

1. Does the firm understand your objectives and expectations?
2. How will results be measured?
3. How will you match your staff to those of the outside consultancy?

Planning the communications function with an external agency

Do's and don'ts of a good client*

1. A communications programme should evolve from a marketing plan. A marketing plan evolves from a business plan. Ensure that you work to planned requirements and don't hire a consultancy just because the chairman wants to see his name in the papers.
2. In choosing an advertising/PR consultancy, ensure that, in terms of budgets, you will be able to use their resources to the full. There is little point in hiring a large 'full service' consultancy if all you will want is the occasional press release.
3. Ensure that any communications programme is seen to have the support of very senior personnel, including the chairman and chief executive. This will ensure that sufficient attention is paid to it by other members of the company.
4. Be sure to devote enough time at the outset of the relationship to establishing a good working rapport and to briefing the consultancy thoroughly. This is time well spent which will provide a good basis for the future.
5. Don't be too subjective. A good solution is not necessarily one that you like – it's one that works for your target audience.
6. Establish a communications structure with the consultancy. Specify those people within your company who will be responsible for implementing the programme in conjunction with the consultancy and ensure that they have sufficient authority and expertise to be able to make decisions.
7. Keep all members of your company informed of the consultancy's work and responsibilities. This will promote a better working relationship and greater co-operation between the two.
8. Use a consultancy as you would a lawyer or a solicitor. It is a specialist in its own right and must be given the opportunity to demonstrate proven skills in its area. Trust your consultancy and work with them as a team.
9. Keep the consultancy informed. This includes developments within your company and its sector. Unless a consultancy is aware

of new business developments, etc., it cannot properly advise on communications with the outside world. The relationship will only work if a two-way stream of communication between client and consultancy is established. In particular, sufficient trust should be built up to enable confidential information to be released to the consultancy. This will ensure that the consultancy has enough time to act on the information before it is generally released.

10. Don't demand unreasonable deadlines from a consultancy. Short notice, especially in the areas of advertising and print, only leads to unsatisfactory work and will inevitably mean higher charges.

11. Be consistent. Set your brief and stick to it. Changes of opinion or direction mean wasted time and money and may lead to the consultancy losing confidence in your commitment.

12. Don't use the consultancy to highlight the deficiencies of other members of your company. In particular don't use a consultancy to undermine existing marketing staff. This will lead to dissatisfaction from all parties and poor results.

13. Most important, remember that you and your consultancy are on the same team.

*This information was prepared by Valin Pollen.

APPENDIX 2

USEFUL ORGANIZATIONS

❧

The Advertising Association
Abford House
15 Wilton Road
London SW1V 1NJ
01-828 2771

Sarah Bayley (Public Affairs Executive)

A federation of 29 trade associations and professional bodies representing advertisers, agencies, the media and support services. The lobbying organization for the UK advertising business on British and European legislative proposals and other issues of common concern, at both national and international levels, and as such campaigns actively to maintain the freedom to advertise and to improve public attitudes to advertising. Publishes UK and European statistics on advertising expenditure, instigates research on advertising issues, and organizes seminars and courses for people in the communications business. Its Information Centre is one of the country's leading sources of advertising and associated subjects.

Association of Exhibition Organisers Ltd (AEO)
1 Totteridge Avenue
High Wycombe
Bucks HP13 6XG
0494 30430

A. Whittle (Administration Director)

Formed in 1920, the Association became a limited company in 1969 and has developed steadily since. It enjoys a substantial membership, and has the reputation of being a leading force in the exhibition industry. Resources have been put into promoting the industry and the interests of members. It organizes a variety of functions for members to exchange views and ideas, and provides a meeting forum. Links have been forged with both Westminster and Whitehall, to focus on the importance of the exhibition industry to the economy.

Association of Free Newspapers (AFN)
Ladybellegate House
Longsmith Street
Gloucester GL1 2HT
0452 26561

Ian Locks (Executive Director)

The organization for publishers of free newspapers and magazines in the United Kingdom. Its main activities are directed to the development of awareness of the free distribution targeted medium as an effective advertising vehicle. It organizes an annual conference, provides a bi-monthly newspaper and quarterly magazine and maintains a database to provide a media planning service for agencies. Services for members include a group libel scheme, regular newsletters and a 'help-line' for legal, employment and personnel, health and safety, and tax investigation advice.

Association of Independent Radio Contractors Ltd (AIRC)
Regina House
259–69 Old Marylebone Road
London NW1 5RA
01-262 6681

Brian West (Director)

The trade association for independent radio. All companies holding franchises awarded by the IBA are members. AIRC provides a forum for the companies and represents their views to the Government, the IBA, trade unions and copyright bodies. It co-ordinates industry programming initiatives such as the Network Chart Show. AIRC's subsidiary, the Radio Marketing Bureau, promotes radio to advertisers and agencies and co-ordinates network advertising activity.

Audit Bureau of Circulations Ltd (ABC)
13 Wimpole Street
London W1M 7AB
01-631 1343

John Holmes (Director)

With a tripartite membership of advertisers, agencies and publishers, ABC is responsible for the certification of circulation and exhibition data provided by independent professional auditors using standard audit procedures. These are accepted by space buyers as authentic. Verified Free Distribution Ltd (same address) is a wholly-owned subsidiary providing a similar service for free publications which cannot be certified under ABC rules which require each copy to be separately wrapped and addressed.

British Association of Industrial Editors Ltd (BAIE)
3 Locks Yard
High Street
Sevenoaks
Kent TN13 1LT
0732 459331

Cecil Pedersen (Chief Executive)

Professional body for persons engaged in corporate communications, public affairs/public relations and in-house publications. The main activities include the Communicator of the Year Award (presented at a luncheon at the Savoy each February), Editing for Industry Awards, an annual study conference and convention held in a different location in the United Kingdom each year, and the monthly publication *BAIE News*.

British Overseas Trade Board (BOTB)
Marketing and Briefing Unit
1–19 Victoria Street
London SW1H 0ET
01-215 4928

Jean Cleary

Guides and directs the export promotion services of the Department of Trade and Industry. The services provide a wide range of assistance to existing and potential exporters in both manufacturing and service industries. Sir James Cleminson is Chairman of the Board and HRH The Duke of Kent is Vice-Chairman. Members are mainly businessmen with practical knowledge of exporting. In addition to the London headquarters, there are ten regional offices throughout the United Kingdom.

British Printing Industries Federation
11 Bedford Row
London WC1R 4DX
01-242 6904

Marion Young (Head of Public Relations)

Has information on over 3,000 member companies and can provide names and addresses in specific printing areas. Guidance and training information are also available.

European Confederation of Public Relations (CERP)
General Secretary
Avenue du Rond-Point 12
B – 1330 Rixensart
Belgium
6 Rosebery Road
London SW2 4DE
01-674 9205

Margaret Nally (Secretary)

Links 16 national professional public relations associations. Formed in 1959, CERP provides contact with more than 13,000 PR practitioners throughout Europe and aims to harmonize professional methods and standards and, for consultants, charging. It provides representation for public relations to the Council of Europe, EEC and UNESCO. Each association has its own national rules and codes but basic CERP codes are respected by all members. CERP is also active in harmonizing PR research, data records and education.

The Communication, Advertising and Marketing
Education Foundation Ltd (CAM Foundation)
Abford House
15 Wilton Road
London SW1V 1NJ
01-828 7506

Donald I. Cole (General Secretary)

The examining body for vocational qualifications in the different functions of communication, set up by 21 institutes and associations who control the nature of each syllabus and the standard of the examinations. CAM qualifications are at two levels – Certificate and Diploma. The entry requirements for the Certificate are equivalent to those for university entrance. Since the Certificate covers the whole area of the UK communication business it is literally an 'industry induction'. The CAM examinations at Diploma level are designed for those who wish to specialize in their chosen career.

Consumers' Association
2 Marylebone Road
London NW1 4DX
01-486 5544

Has over a million members. Publishes *Which?* and many useful books. Campaigns on special and selected issues.

Design Council
28 Haymarket
London SW1Y 4SU
01-839 8000

Deborah Hale (Publicity Officer)

A government-funded organization to encourage and promote the improvement of design in the products of British industry. It provides advice to companies on the solution of design problems through the Design Advisory Service and Support for Design Scheme; produces the *Designer Directory*, a comprehensive list and recommendation service for design skills in Britain; publishes books and magazines, including *Design* and *Engineering*.

Direct Mail Producers Association (DMPA)
34 Grand Avenue
London N10 3BP
01-883 7229

Karen Naylor (Assistant Director)

The trade association for agencies engaged in direct mail activities on behalf of their clients. There are currently over 100 member companies. It can provide advice to advertisers who are contemplating the use of direct mail or who are seeking specialist support. It handles some 3,000 enquiries a year.

Friends of the Earth
23–26 Underwood Street
London N1 7JQ
01-490 1555

Environment organization of active campaigners on selected environmental issues.

Incorporated Society of British Advertisers Ltd (ISBA)
44 Hertford Street
London W1Y 8AE
01-499 7502

Kenneth Miles (Director)

The only organization which exclusively represents the interests and needs of 'client companies', for whom advertising is an important element in their marketing plans. ISBA membership includes most leading companies, many being international groups based outside Britain. ISBA priorities include contact with government and the media on behalf of advertisers, and advice to companies on key practical subjects. Sponsorship, public relations and exhibitions are also covered, with corporate communication as important as product advertising.

Independent Broadcasting Authority (IBA)
70 Brompton Road
London SW3 1EY
01-584 7011

Miss S. M. Fewell (Senior Information Assistant)

Independent Television (ITV and Channel 4) regularly attracts the greater share of the available viewing audience and its programmes have also earned an enviable reputation overseas. Together with Independent Local Radio (ILR), these services are completely self-supporting, deriving their income from the sale of spot advertising time. The IBA is the public body responsible for the organization and supervision of the system as a whole and for seeing that programmes and schedules are in accordance with the provisions of the Broad-casting Act 1981.

Independent Television Companies Association Ltd (ITCA)
Knighton House
56 Mortimer Street
London W1N 8AN
01-636 6866

D. Shaw (General Secretary)

The central body serving the needs of the 16 independent television contractors currently operating in the United Kingdom. The Association undertakes on behalf of its members those activities which need to be handled or co-ordinated centrally. General matters are dealt with by the Central Secretariat and a number of standing committees exist to deal with specific areas re programming, marketing, public relations and industrial relations.

Institute of Directors
116 Pall Mall
London SW1Y 5ED
01-839 1233

Gordon Leak (Public Relations Director)

Founded in 1903, it is the largest representative business organization committed to the defence and promotion of free enterprise. It aims to provide an effective voice to represent the interests of its members; to bring the experience of the business leader to bear on the conduct of public affairs for the common good and to encourage and help its members to improve their professional competence as business leaders. Its members are directors of public and private companies, partners and professional men and women.

Institute of Export
Export House
64 Clifton Street
London EC2A 4HB
01-247 9812

M. L. Sansom (Director, International Services)

A professional association for managers and companies engaged in overseas trade, incorporated in 1935. It seeks to set and raise the standards of export practice and management through formal and informal education and the exchange of ideas and information between members. It publishes a journal (ten issues per year), operates a staff bureau and export specialists' service, represents members' views to the Government and provides an information service.

Institute of Marketing (IM)
Moor Hall
Cookham
Maidenhead
Berks SL6 9QH
062 85 24922

Jenny Hellmuth (Marketing Assistant)

Founded in 1911, it is the largest marketing advisory and training organization in Europe. Its primary function is to increase the level of awareness and understanding of marketing as a vital factor in business success and to stimulate enhanced marketing performance throughout commerce and industry in the United Kingdom. It undertakes research into business and is involved with the Government and other influential bodies in bringing the benefits of marketing excellence to the attention of industry and commerce via conferences, political lobbying, the media and the membership itself. Total membership is 22,000 and IM is the largest single professional body in the world concerned with marketing.

Institute of Practitioners in Advertising (IPA)
44 Belgrave Square
London SW1X 8QS
01-235 7020

David Wheeler (Director General)

The professional and trade organization for UK advertising agencies. It represents the collective view of agencies and the people who work in them, in discussions and negotiations with government departments, the media, and industry and consumer organizations. It also makes an important contribution to the effective operation of advertising agencies through its advisory, training and information services. There are 250 member agencies (as well as over 1,400 personal members) who between them handle over 80 per cent of all advertising placed by UK agencies.

Institute of Public Relations (IPR)
Gate House
1 St John's Square
London EC1M 4DH
01-253 5151

J. B. Lavelle (Executive Director)

Represents and regulates professional practitioners in the United Kingdom. It was founded in 1948 and is by far the largest organization of its kind in Europe. Its concern is to maintain and raise the standard of professional practice, so ensuring that public relations practice achieves and deserves status, recognition and understanding.

Institute of Trading Standards Administration
Thamesgate House
Suite 18
37 Victoria Avenue
Southend on Sea
Essex SS2 6BU
0702 338313

The professional body for Trading Standards Officers, who investigate complaints and enforce laws relating to false or misleading descriptions or prices, inaccurate weights and measures, and some aspects of the safety of goods and of consumer credit.

International Association of Business Communicators (IABC)
Eagle House
110 Jermyn Street
London SW1Y 6HA
01-839 3086

Marian Hawkins

An American-based organization for over 10,000 employee relations and public affairs managers, writers, audio-visual specialists, consultants and others who are involved or interested in organizational communication. The UK branch was established in 1979 and runs workshops, seminars and social events. The IABC publishes an international monthly magazine and the UK branch publishes its own newsletter. An annual convention is held.

International Public Relations Association (IPRA)
Case Postale 126
CH–1211 Geneva 20
Switzerland
+41 22 910 550

Anthony J. Murdoch (Secretary General)

Founded in 1955, it is a professional organization, dedicated to high standards of practice and mutual understanding between groups, organizations and nations.

Market Research Society (MRS)
175 Oxford Street
London W1R 1TA
01-439 2585

John Hosker (Director-General)

The professional body for market research practitioners. It administers the Diploma in Market Research (the only professional qualification solely concerned with market research) and has an extensive programme of other training courses, which are open to nonmembers. The Society produces a range of publications dealing with market research. It was established in 1946 and has 5,500 members.

National Association of Citizens Advice Bureaux
Myddelton House
115–23 Pentonville Road
London N1 9LZ
01-833 2181

Over 1000 outlets throughout the United Kingdom provide the consumer with wide-ranging information, advice and assistance.

National Consumer Council
20 Grosvenor Gardens
London SW1W 0DE
01-730 3469

An independent specialist organization with government funding. Its job is to speak up for the users of goods and services of all kinds.

Office of Fair Trading
Field House
Breams Buildings
London EC4 1PR
01-242 2858

Concerned with the conduct of trade and industry in the United Kingdom, whether large or small. It deals with consumer credit monopolies and mergers as well as with restrictive practices. The office also publishes useful consumer advice and literature.

Public Relations Consultants Association
Premier House
10 Greycoat Place
London SW1P 1SB
01-222 8866

C. G. Thompson (Secretary General)

The trade association for public relations consultancies. Formed in 1968, it represents over 80 per cent of consultancies in terms of fee income. Members have to conform to a strict code of practice. It represents members with the Government, commercial bodies and education and training bodies. It also sponsors awards for outstanding consultancy practice. It provides training literature, workshops and seminars, and encourages the development of business through management documents. It provides potential clients with a simple selection system through a computer matrix and is always available to give advice.

Society of Consumer Affairs Professionals in Business (SOCAP)
London House
53–54 Haymarket
London SW1Y 4RP
01-930 4241

A professional organization of individuals whose purpose is to foster and maintain the integrity of business in dealings with consumers, encourage and promote effective communications and understanding between business, Government and consumers, and to define and advance the consumer affairs profession. SOCAP was founded in 1973 in the United States and the UK society was founded in 1985. SOCAP UK has just over 100 member companies from various sectors, e.g. retailers, manufacturers, the motor trade, travel, leisure and financial institutions, as well as specialist consumer affairs consultancies.

APPENDIX 3

USEFUL MEDIA

℮≈℮

(a) Journals

Achievement
World Trade Magazines Ltd
World Trade House
145 High Street
Sevenoaks
Kent TN13 1XJ
0732 458144

Achievement is a magazine devoted to reporting on major international capital projects.

Broadcast
100 Avenue Road
Swiss Cottage
London NW3 3TP
01-935 6611

Important weekly for the broadcasting industry.

Conference Britain
International Trade Publications Ltd
Queensway House
2 Queensway
Redhill
Surrey RH1 1QS
0737 68611

The leading UK magazine for organizers of conferences, exhibitions, meetings and incentive travel.

Campaign
22 Lancaster Road
London W2 3LY
01-402 4200

The key weekly for the advertising industry, it also covers related issues.

Design
The Design Council
28 Haymarket
London SW1Y 4SU
01-839 8000

Informs managers and designers about industrial design.

Director
The Director Publications Ltd
10 Belgrave Square
London SW1X 8PH
01-235 9122

Leading monthly magazine for chief executives, directors and businessmen.

Marketing
22 Lancaster Gate
London W2 3LY
01-402 4200

Important weekly for the marketing industry.

Marketing Week
60 Kingley Street
London W1R 5LH
01-439 4222

Important weekly covering marketing and related areas.

Media Week
20–22 Wellington Street
London WC2E 7DD
01-240 9851

Relatively new and influential weekly covering media matters.

PR Week
100 Fleet Street
London EC4Y 1DE
01-353 9804

The PR business weekly – read in the main by PR practitioners in consultancies and in-house departments.

US Press Gazette
Bouverie Publishing
244–49 Temple Chambers
Temple Avenue
London EC4Y 0DT
01-583 6463

Influential publication read in the main by journalists.

(b) Reference books

Advertiser's Annual
Thomas Skinner Directories
Windsor Court
East Grinstead
West Sussex RH19 1XE
0342 26972

British Rate and Data
76 Oxford Street
London W1N 0MM

Benn's Media Directory
Benn Business Information Services Ltd
PO Box 20
Sovereign Way
Tonbridge
Kent TN9 1RQ
0732 362666

Hollis Press & Public Relations Annual
Contact House
Lower Hampton Road
Sunbury-on-Thames
Middlesex TW16 5HG
09327 84781

Public Relations Year Book
PRCA
Premier House
10 Greycoat Place
London SW1P 1SB
01-222 8866

Published by The Financial Times Business Information, this is the official year book for the Public Relations Consultants Association. It lists member companies and gives details of company structure; it also includes full client lists on an annual and ad hoc basis. In addition it contains some case histories and other useful reference material as well as the PRCA Code of Consultancy Practice.

APPENDIX 4

PRESS CUTTING AGENCIES

❧

Durrants Press Cuttings Ltd
103 Whitecross Street
London EC1Y 8QT
01-588 3671

International Press Cutting Bureau
70 Newington Causeway
London SE17 1JE
01-708 2113

Media Scan Ltd
Northgate House
2 Scrutton Street
London EC2A 4RJ
01-247 5513

News Clip (UK)
52–53 Fetter Lane
London EC4A 1BL
01-353 7191

Romeike & Curtice Ltd
Hale House
290–96 Green Lanes
London N13 5TP
01-882 0155

Timms Press Information Ltd
151 Fleet Street
London EC4A 2DQ
01-583 7585

APPENDIX 5

NEWS AND FEATURE DISTRIBUTION

ᥫᦰ

PNA Medialink
13–19 Curtain Road
London EC2A 3LT
01-377 2521

Press Association Ltd
85 Fleet Street
London EC4P 4BE
01-353 7440

Regional News Agency
Room 303
32–36 Fleet Street
London EC4
01-236 2650

Reuters Ltd
85 Fleet Street
London EC4P 4AJ
01-250 1122

Tass News Agency
Communications House
Gough Square
London EC4A 3JH
01-353 9831

Universal News Services
Communications House
Gough Square
London EC4P 4DP
01-353 5200

APPENDIX 6

RESEARCH ORGANIZATIONS

୧≈୬

Market and Opinion Research International Ltd (MORI)
32 Old Queen Street
London SW1H 9HP
01-222 0232

Schlackmans
32 St John's Wood Road
London NW8 7HB
01-289 3431

Taylor Nelson Group
457 Kingston Road
Ewell
Epsom
Surrey KT19 0DH
01-394 0191

APPENDIX 7

AGENCY AND CONSULTANCY
SELECTION SERVICES

☙

Advertising Agency Register
62 Shaftesbury Avenue
London W1V 7DE
01-434 2970

PR Selection
40 Ravenscourt Gardens
Hammersmith
London W6 0TU
01-748 1783

Public Relations Register
62 Shaftesbury Avenue
London W1V 7DE
01-437 3357

APPENDIX 8

CODES OF PRACTICE

౸

THERE are several Codes of Practice of importance and relevance in corporate communication. Some of these and the organizations concerned are listed below.

British Code of Advertising Practice
Code of Advertising Practice Committee
Brook House
2–16 Torrington Place
London WC1E 7HN

British Code of Sales Promotion Practice
Code of Advertising Practice Committee
Brook House
2–16 Torrington Place
London WC1E 7HN

IBA Code of Advertising Standards and Practice
Independent Broadcasting Authority
70 Brompton Road
London SW3 1EY

Public Relations Consultants Association Code of Consultancy Practice
Public Relations Consultants Association
Premier House
10 Greycoat Place
London SW1P 1SB

INDEX

୧∾୨